Surprises

Alan Ayckbourn was born in London in 1939 to a violinist father and a mother who was a writer. He left school at seventeen with two 'A' levels and went straight into the theatre. Two years in regional theatre as an actor and stage manager led in 1959 to the writing of his first play, *The Square Cat*, for Scarborough's Theatre in the Round at the instigation of his then employer and subsequent mentor, Stephen Joseph. Some 76 plays later, his work has been translated into over 35 languages, is performed on stage and television throughout the world and has won countless awards. There have been English and French screen adaptations, the most notable being Alain Resnais' fine film of *Private Fears in Public Places*.

Major successes include *Relatively Speaking*, *How the Other Half Loves*, *Absurd Person Singular*, *Bedroom Farce*, *A Chorus of Disapproval*, *The Norman Conquests*, *A Small Family Business*, *Henceforward . . .*, *Comic Potential*, *Things We Do for Love*, *Life of Riley* and *Neighbourhood Watch*. In 2009, he retired as Artistic Director of the Stephen Joseph Theatre, where almost all his plays have been and continue to be first staged, after 37 years in the post. Knighted in 1997 for services to the theatre, he received the 2010 Critics' Circle Award for Services to the Arts and became the first British playwright to receive both Olivier and Tony Special Lifetime Achievement Awards.

by the same author

WOMAN IN MIND (DECEMBER BEE)
MR A'S AMAZING MAZE PLAYS
INVISIBLE FRIENDS
TIME OF MY LIFE
WILDEST DREAMS
COMMUNICATING DOORS
COMIC POTENTIAL
THE BOY WHO FELL INTO A BOOK
WHENEVER
DAMSELS IN DISTRESS
THE JOLLIES
MY SISTER SADIE
SEASON'S GREETINGS

ALAN AYCKBOURN: PLAYS ONE
(*A Chorus of Disapproval, A Small Family Business, Henceforward . . . , Man of the Moment*)

ALAN AYCKBOURN: PLAYS TWO
(*Ernie's Incredible Illucinations, Invisible Friends, This Is Where We Came In, My Very Own Story, The Champion of Paribanou*)

ALAN AYCKBOURN: PLAYS THREE
(*Haunting Julia, Sugar Daddies, Drowning on Dry Land, Private Fears in Public Places*)

ALAN AYCKBOURN: PLAYS FOUR
(*The Revengers' Comedies, Things We Do for Love, House & Garden*)

ALAN AYCKBOURN: PLAYS FIVE
(*Snake in the Grass, If I Were You, Life and Beth, My Wonderful Day, Life of Riley*)

adaptations
THE FOREST by Alexander Ostrovsky

theatre books
THE CRAFTY ART OF PLAYMAKING

ALAN AYCKBOURN

Surprises

THREE LINKED ROMANCES

faber and faber

First published in 2012
by Faber and Faber Limited
74–77 Great Russell Street, London WC1B 3DA

Typeset by Country Setting, Kingsdown, Kent CT14 8ES
Printed in England by CPI Group (UK) Ltd, Croydon, CR0 4YY

A CIP record for this book
is available from the British Library

ISBN 978–0–571–29766–5

2 4 6 8 10 9 7 5 3 1

Surprises, a co-production between the Stephen Joseph Theatre and Chichester Festival Theatre, was first presented at the Stephen Joseph Theatre, Scarborough, on 17 July 2012, and subsequently at the Minerva Theatre, Chichester, on 13 August 2012. The cast, in alphabetical order, was as follows:

Grace / Seraphina Ayesha Antoine
Franklin Bill Champion
Sylvia / Zandy Laura Doddington
Lorraine / Inez / Bellina Sarah Parks
Titus / Conrad Ben Porter
Jan / Gorman Richard Stacey

Director Alan Ayckbourn
Designer Michael Holt
Lighting Designer Jason Taylor
Casting Director Sarah Hughes CDG

Note

Many of the characters in these plays are non-human, either android or virtual holographic creations. Moreover, several of the human characters are of considerably advanced years. However, owing to continuing advances in cosmetic and geriatric surgery, they are all, in appearance, remarkably well preserved for their age.

Characters

ONE: THE SURPRISE HUSBAND
Grace's bedroom. Sometime soon.

Grace
aged sixteen

Franklin
her father, aged seventy

Gorman
a tour guide with TLT, subsequently HEA,
aged in his thirties

Titus
a tourist with TLT/HEA aged sixty-eight
(and voice of Tim, aged eighteen)

Inez
a tourist with TLT/HEA, aged in her fifties
(doubling Lorraine)

Zandy
her friend, another tourist with TLT/HEA,
aged in her fifties (doubling Sylvia)

TWO: THE SURPRISE BIRTHDAY
Lorraine's office. Sometime soon. The same day.

Lorraine
a lawyer, aged sixty

Sylvia
her secretary, aged thirty

Franklin
her client, a retired executive, aged seventy

Conrad
her husband, aged forty
(doubling Titus)

Jan Sixty
a security/maintenance android
(doubling Gorman)

THREE: SURPRISES
Sylvia's office / Titus's office / a virtual bar.
Fifty years from then.

Sylvia
a PA, aged eighty

Titus
an executive with HEA, aged sixty-eight

Franklin
his father-in-law, MD of HEA,
aged one hundred and twenty

Grace
Titus's wife, aged sixty-six

Lorraine
a retired lawyer, aged one hundred and ten

Jan Sixty
an android, her partner

'Seraphina'
Sylvia's avatar
(doubling Grace)

'Fabiano'
Titus's avatar
(doubling Jan)

'Bellina'
a virtual barmaid
(doubling Lorraine)

SURPRISES

One

THE SURPRISE HUSBAND

Grace's bedroom. Sometime soon.

It is a good-sized, luxurious teenager's bedroom, even by the latest standards.

Two doors, one to the landing, the other to an en-suite bathroom.

Grace is sitting on the large bed, playing with an old, favourite toy of hers, a Playboy. She throws it from time to time in the air. Each time she does so the doll emits a cry of joy. She seems only half aware she is doing this, but maybe it is to irritate her father, Franklin, standing unhappily some distance from her, getting increasingly irritated by this.

A long silence between them. Grace throws the toy in the air three times.

Franklin (*at length*) And that's your final word, is it, Grace?

Grace throws the toy and catches it again but does not react.

That's what you want me to tell your mother? You won't even consider waiting until you're . . . at least till you're seventeen?

Silence. Grace throws the toy and catches it.

(*Pacing around unhappily*) I mean, I'm stuck in the middle here, Grace. See it from my point of view, can't you, darling? Your mother . . . she's . . . Martha is . . . she's – very opposed to this, you know . . . You know that.

Silence. Grace throws the toy and catches it.

It doesn't help that you refuse to speak to each other. I mean, if you only talked, now and again, you and your mother . . . from time to time . . . But you're both so alike. Once you make up your minds, you're . . .

Silence. Grace throws the toy twice more.

She loves you, Grace. She does. She worries about you. She's your mother. Mothers worry about their daughters. They watch them – gradually growing into – women. And they worry. Women especially – worry about women.

Grace (*shaking her head, scornfully*) Oh, Dad!

She throws the toy in the air again. This time Franklin is close enough to her to intercept it before she can catch it again.

Franklin (*losing patience*) Oh, come on, Grace, for God's sake!

Irritably, he throws the Playboy on the floor. It gives a little cry of dismay.

You have to cut me a bit of slack here, please!

Grace What? *Slack?*

Franklin (*vaguely*) Slack. It's – er . . . it means . . . sort of loose, you know . . . allow me a bit of loose . . . (*Giving up*) So what am I going to tell your mother? That you refuse point blank to consider it? Waiting till she gets back? You refuse to give him up, this boy? This workman? This untrained labourer?

Grace Tim's fully qualified and skilled . . . I keep saying –

Franklin Grace, he's not even trained. I had him checked out. He's a trainee.

Grace He's learning on the job! He's learning from experience!

Franklin He's sub-android level. Grade Two education. He never even made Grade Three.

Grace So? I barely made Grade Three either, did I?

Franklin You're different – you've got – us . . . your mother and me . . .

Grace Meaning money?

Franklin It's different when you're – when you're educated privately . . .

Grace Yes, money . . .

Franklin . . . you have Jemima, she's –

Grace . . . I have money! Money, money!

Franklin I've told you before, never sneer at money, Grace.

Grace It's not important! Not for me, it isn't.

Franklin It's not important till it matters. Then you'll soon find it becomes the only thing that does matter.

Grace shrugs.

He's no better than an android, Grace. No, he's lower than an android. He's cleaning up after androids.

Grace You shouldn't talk about androids like that. Not these days. Some of them have built-in feelings, you know . . .

Franklin Oh, well, pardon me, I'm sure. In my day we didn't feel honour bound to be polite to labour-saving machines . . . I do beg their pardon.

Grace Dad!

Franklin I'm seventy-one years old next birthday, Grace . . . Forgive me for being old-fashioned . . .

Grace (*throwing herself back on the bed, mimicking Franklin*) 'I've seen over six decades in my lifetime, my girl . . .'

Franklin Grace, come on now . . .

Grace (*continuing*) '. . . I can remember when there was grass growing where the concrete used to be . . .'

Franklin Grace . . .

Grace (*remorselessly*) '. . . *real* grass, I'll have you know, right up to here . . .'

Franklin (*quite sharply, for him*) Grace, will you stop that!

She stops. A silence.

Just stop it!

Grace (*sulkily*) Sorry.

Franklin We used to respect our parents, at least. When your mother and I were young . . .

Grace (*her eyes still closed, murmuring*) . . . back in the good old days . . .

Franklin What?

Grace Nothing.

Franklin We had respect . . . We listened. We learnt. Sometimes. At least we had the courtesy to listen.

Silence.

Look, if we don't get this sorted out before your mother comes back, there'll be hell. I spoke to her this morning and she's – angry and upset at your attitude. Putting it mildly. She was two hundred and twenty-five million kilometres away, I could actually feel the heat coming off her. She's a determined woman, your mother, Grace.

Grace So am I.

Franklin Yes . . .

Grace Like you said, you're trapped between us, Dad. That's no place to be, I warn you. Sooner or later you're going to have to choose sides.

Franklin I hope it won't come to that.

Grace (*grimly*) Me or Mum. Make up your mind.

Slight pause.

Franklin Well, a few more months, she'll be back with us.

Grace She's been gone ages. Five and a half years. She'll barely remember me, will she?

Franklin Nonsense.

Grace When she went away, I was only ten and a half.

Franklin If you'd only talk to her sometimes . . .

Grace I'd talk to her if she was here to talk to . . .

Franklin You can use the Vislink.

Grace Vislinking's not the same.

Franklin I tell you, the Vislink's pretty good these days. Especially interplanetary. Much more reliable than it used to be.

Grace There's still those gaps. (*Mimicking*) 'How are you, dear?' (*Denoting the delay time*) Duh-duh-duh-duh-duh . . . 'Fine, Mum' . . . Duh-duh-duh-duh-duh . . . 'Oh, good, dear' . . . Duh-duh-duh-duh-duh . . . (*Irritably*) What's she doing there all this time, anyway?

Franklin Don't ask me, some big construction project, I don't know. I don't envy her. That's no place to be stuck for any length of time, believe me.

Grace I'd like to go. One day.

Franklin Really?

Grace Have you ever been?

Franklin Mars? Once. Briefly. Years ago. I was space-sick for six months, all the way there. And then again all the way back. While I was there they discovered I suffered from GDD. Gravity Deficiency Disorder. My first and last trip into space. These days I leave it to your mother.

Grace Do you miss her?

Franklin Yes, I do. She drives me crazy half the time when she's here. When she's away, I can't sleep for worrying about her.

Grace What, Mum? You worry about *Mum*?

Franklin Well, accidents happen – occasionally. Let's face it, it's not a natural life for a woman, is it? Hurtling around the solar system with a toolbox? No, of course I miss her. I still love her. I love both of you, Grace. As we both love you. And if you go ahead with this boy, it'll break her heart.

Grace If I don't, it'll break mine, I warn you.

A silence as they reach the same impasse.

Anyway, you weren't that much older than I am when you first met her, were you? What age was Mum when you met?

Franklin That was long ago. Different times, Grace, different circumstances . . .

Grace What age was she?

Franklin (*reluctantly*) Seventeen. (*Smiling*) Fifty-two years ago next month. Five fifteen p.m. We met on the promenade.

Grace Where was that?

Franklin Doesn't matter, it's long gone. Some east coast town that fell into the sea years ago . . . We were both students . . . I was on vacation working at the fairground . . . You're too young to remember fairgrounds . . . they were fun . . . All closed down by Health and Safety long ago. She was on holiday, she and her friend . . . I was working The Collider . . . (*With relish*) Yes! Sweet-talked me into giving them free rides . . . she and I fell in love . . . she proposed . . . ran away together . . . married a few weeks later.

Grace She proposed?

Franklin She knew what she wanted, even in those days.

Grace What did your parents say when they found out you'd married?

Franklin Not much. Father was too busy to listen, Mother was too drunk to care.

Grace What about her parents?

Franklin Martha wasn't on the best of terms with them, I seem to recall.

Grace But none of them stood in your way? They didn't try to stop you, did they?

Franklin I don't think they really cared either way, Grace. Just relieved to get us off their hands. Parents back in those days were . . . more selfish. You need to understand that children were a – a far less valued commodity than they are today. In those days kids were ten a penny. Everywhere you looked – kids. The point is, we do care, Martha and I. You're very precious to us. You have to understand, we need to know that you're absolutely certain, that's all. We don't want you to be hurt, darling.

Grace I'm certain . . . I've never been . . . (*Suddenly crying*) I can't lose him, Dad . . . I want him . . . he's everything . . . everything to me . . . please! Please say yes . . . You have to say yes . . . please . . .

Franklin, somewhat startled at this abrupt change in her mood, holds her in his arms gently. Grace clings to him, crying. Maybe she's trying it on, maybe she isn't. It certainly weakens Franklin.

Franklin Now, Grace! Alright . . . it's alright . . . darling . . . it's alright . . .

Grace (*still in his arms*) Sorry, I didn't mean to cry on you. I promised myself I was going to be grown-up about this . . . I'm sorry . . .

Franklin . . . that's alright . . . don't be sorry . . .

Grace (*pulling herself together*) Sorry. Better now. Grown-up again. (*Sniffing*) There. Tim's not going to be a labourer for ever, you know, Dad. He has plans. He's got great plans. He's not even going to need my money. Not by the time he's finished. He's – (*She sniffs again*) Sorry, I need to get a wipe. Excuse me . . .

Grace goes off to the bathroom. We hear the door close.

Franklin stands for a moment staring after his daughter, shaking his head. When he's sure Grace is out of earshot, he double taps his ear to connect his inbuilt communicator. He waits for a reply.

Franklin (*in a new, sharper tone*) Lorraine? . . . Yes. Go ahead, please. Set it up immediately . . . Yes, as soon as possible. Make the offer . . . Yes . . . Yes, no higher, no . . . That's maximum. I'll be along later . . .

He taps his ear to disconnect as Grace returns to catch him ending his call.

Checking to see if there's any vocal messages from your mother. She's out of range. Probably down a Martian mineshaft. How about you? How are you planning to spend today? Seeing Tim?

Grace He's working today. I may do a dance class, later on . . .

Franklin Perhaps you could do a little work, darling? Some school work?

Grace I can't. Jemima's being reprogrammed.

Franklin Oh, yes, so she is.

Grace She's not being delivered back till tomorrow.

Franklin Yes, I remember now. The technician called me. He said that someone had been asking Jemima – inappropriate questions – as he put it. He reckons that's what caused the overload.

Grace (*innocently*) Really?

Franklin Was that you?

Grace What? Was what me?

Franklin Were you asking your auto-governess inappropriate questions?

Grace I don't know what you mean. What's inappropriate?

Franklin Well . . .

Grace She's a teacher, isn't she? Teachers ought to know everything. I mean, what's the point of a teacher who doesn't know everything? I'm growing up, I'm a woman. I need to know things, Dad.

Franklin (*embarrassed*) Well, I'm sure we can find some human to – to discuss –

Grace No, not *those* things. I know all about that, I learnt all about *that* years ago. I mean emotional stuff. You know, feelings. Sometimes, I have these feelings, you know . . . I get so . . . Oh, forget it, Dad, you wouldn't understand. You're a man.

Franklin (*unhappily*) If you'd only talk to your mother . . . This'd be so much easier for me to handle, Grace. If only she'd give up work. She doesn't need to work.

Grace You ever going to get another job?

Franklin Well, you never know, I've started sounding around. After twenty years you get restless. Long time to be retired. (*Making to move*) Well, I must . . . go and see if the household's still running . . . Our beloved butler's developed a system fault again . . .

Grace Adolf? What's he doing now?

Franklin Keeps mixing and then serving up expensive drinks that nobody's asked for and then having a tantrum and throwing them into the swimming pool. Machines! I tell you. Designed to save you time. End up costing you a fortune.

Grace Never mind, Dad, it's only money . . .

Franklin moves to the door.

Dad, for the tenth time, could you possibly delete my personal protocols from the House Computer? I keep asking you. It's so embarrassing – all my friends laugh at me –

Franklin Now, I've told you before, that's down to your mother, darling. She's the one who put them on. I don't even know her pass code. You'll have to ask her . . .

Grace You know her pass code, you can delete them easily . . .

Franklin Your mother'll be back soon. Ask her.

Grace Well, at least remove them with the servants. They won't fetch me anything unless I say *please*. Then they won't give it to me until I've said thank you, *thank you*. Practically have to grovel.

Franklin Ah, well, you know what your mother would say, don't you? . . . 'Apart from "I love you", the three little words which bring most –'

Grace '– which bring most joy in this world are "please" and "thank you".'

Franklin Exactly. That's what she'd say.

Grace All my friends laugh at me.

Franklin Then your friends are all wrong, darling.

Grace The servants laugh at me, too.

Franklin No . . .

Grace They do! I've heard them! Laughing! Behind my back!

Franklin They're not programmed to laugh at you, Grace, whatever next?

Grace My maid does! Maxie does. I heard her. I was getting dressed in front of the mirror, there . . . Just – looking at myself, you know. She was laughing. At me! She was! I caught her!

Franklin I think you're just getting a little tiny bit paranoid, darling . . . It's called growing up. See you later on.

Franklin goes out.

Grace (*shouting after him, angrily*) Maybe I wouldn't be paranoid if I was allowed to grow up normally! If you and Mum didn't treat me like a f— (*She winces and clasps her head, more in anger than in pain*) – Ow! Ow! Ow!

She lies back on the bed.

(*Muttering*) Not even allowed to swear, am I? All my friends are allowed to swear.

She lies sulking for a little while.

(*Addressing the ceiling*) Locate Tim. (*After a pause, sourly*) Please.

A beep.
She is immediately connected. A background din of industrial machinery.

Tim (*his voice, over the background*) Hallo, Gracious.

Grace Where are you?

Tim (*his voice*) Working on site. Clearing all this – junk . . .

Grace Wish I could see you.

Tim (*his voice*) I'm at work, Gracious. You know I can't afford a personal Vislink.

Grace I said, I'd buy you one. I want to see you. I need to see you, Gorgeous!

Tim (*his voice*) I can see you.

Grace (*squirming provocatively*) Yes? What do you see?

Tim (*his voice*) Hey! Is that the bed? I want to climb in there with you, Gracious.

Grace I'm here, what are you waiting for?

Tim (*his voice, laughing*) What have you been doing then, Gracious? Apart from lying in bed all day?

Grace Nothing much. Watched a bit of Conrad Cato . . .

Tim (*his voice*) Conrad Cato? What you doing watching him? He's terrible.

Grace Yes, well, he can be quite funny. Sometimes. He wasn't today. And then I've been talking to Dad, you know . . . about us . . .

Tim (*his voice, more serious*) And? What's he say?

Grace Still the same. They're not even prepared to listen. Either of them.

Tim (*his voice*) Well, give them time . . .

Grace (*petulantly*) We've given them time. I want you now, Gorgeous. *Now!*

There is no response.

Tim? Tim? Are you there?

Tim (*his voice*) Hang on, Gracious – just helping – (*With an effort, to someone else*) Hah! You got it, then?

Various clunks and bumps. Grace waits impatiently.

Sure? Right! . . . Two – three . . . Letting go – hup! Sorry, Gracious, back with you now . . .

Grace Don't work too hard . . . Save something for later . . .

Tim (*his voice*) I'm stopping in a minute . . . Fizz just phoned . . . he says he's just had a call from someone . . . all that networking we've been doing, it's paid off, Gracious. We've had a reply at last . . . We finally got a bite. Someone's finally interested . . .

Grace Wonderful. Who is it?

Tim (*his voice*) No idea. Some lawyer. She wants to meet up with us both later on. Fizz said she sounded very interested. Extremely keen.

Grace Well, be careful. You know how Fizz gets. Excited over anything.

Tim (*his voice*) He's a genius, Gracious. I tell you, we have to trust him. All Fizz needs is opportunity. A little tender financial encouragement . . . some loving support . . .

Grace Yes, maybe. I love you, Gorgeous. Not Fizz. It's you I love. You!

Tim (*his voice*) You keep it that way, Gracious. (*As the background sounds increase*) Because I tell you you're the only one . . . (*His voice starting to break up*) . . . I've ever . . . truly . . . if I ever lost you . . . I don't know . . . probably throw myself off . . .

Grace Tim? You there?

Tim (*his voice, in a final burst*) . . . Sorry, Gracious, got to go . . . talk to you later . . .

The connection cuts off abruptly. A beep.
Silence. Grace lies sulking.

Grace (*at length, to the ceiling*) Music. Random.

Silence.

Please.

A beep. The room is filled with loud contemporary popular music.

(*Sharply*) No! Not that!

The music continues.

(*More politely*) Not that, *please*!

Another beep. The room is silent again.

Music. Mood match, pleeeease.

Another beep.
Quieter, slower, classical ballet music. Grace lies back, eyes closed, practising half-hearted dance movements.

A whooshing sound like a vacuum suddenly filling with air as a group of figures appears to materialise in one corner of the room. It is a group of time travellers conveyed there presumably by a time machine, though that is not visible to the naked eye.

Leading the group is the tour guide, Gorman. He wears his distinctive uniform jacket with its TLT logo. He is escorting three tourists, Inez, Zandy and Titus. It is the women's first tour with Time Leap Tours and they are clearly excited. Titus, middle-aged, casually but expensively dressed, stands quietly apart from them. Their voices sound slightly boxy from being inside the closed Time Bubble. Grace continues with her horizontal ballet unaware of them.

Inez
Zandy (*as they arrive, shrieking, as if on a big dipper*) Eeeeeee!

Gorman Hold tight there, please! (*Cheerfully*) Sorry, should have warned you, folks, pulling out of the recent stream, it can get a little bumpy.

Zandy (*clasping her chest*) Oh, my heart!

Inez Is it always going to be like that?

Gorman Not at all. As I was explaining, this is an ROS. What we call a Recent Occurrence Stop. With an ROS, the temporal stream's still comparatively turbulent. The further back we get from our Initial Occasion – remember I explained to you about Initial Occasion – the further back we get, the wider the stream and the less temporal turbulence there tends to be . . .

Zandy It's all way beyond me, this, you know. Do you understand him, Inez?

Inez Not a word, I gave up trying back there.

Gorman Listen, you need to think of it a bit like a river . . .

Zandy Better not! I can't swim!

Inez Nor can I!

Both women go off into paroxysms of laughter.

Gorman (*wearily, to himself*) Oh dear, oh dear . . .

For him, it is going to be a long trip at this rate. He presses a button which opens the Bubble's portal. The women's laughter fills the bedroom. Grace sits up and regards them in open-mouthed surprise.

Grace (*finding her voice, indignantly*) I say, excuse me . . .

Inez and Zandy continue laughing.

Hey! Hey! Hey! OY! (*Louder*) I said excuse me! HEY, YOU LOT!!

The laughter stops. The travellers look at her.

What are you doing? Would you kindly tell me what you're doing here?

Inez Oh!

Zandy Can she hear us?

Inez I didn't realise she could hear us.

Gorman Oh, yes. She can hear you. Once the portal's open. I've just opened the portal, you see . . .

Inez I didn't realise . . .

Grace (*wincing every time she attempts to swear*) Of course, I can hear you! What the – ow! – are you doing in my – ow! – bedroom? You – bunch of – ow – ow!

Inez Oh, isn't it beautiful?!

Zandy Lovely room!

Inez Lucky girl, isn't she?

Grace Look, will you just – ow! – off, you stupid – ow – ow! (*She clutches her head and lies back*) Ow . . . Please God, let me swear. Just once!

Inez Ah! Look at her! Sweet little thing . . .

Zandy You alright, sweetheart?

Grace Ow – off!

Gorman Sorry, ladies, this is a special stop just to allow this gentleman to disembark. If you'd step aside, please. This way, Mr Titus.

The women are gently moved aside to allow Titus through.

Titus Thank you.

Inez Oh, is he getting off, then?

Titus Thank you.

Zandy Can we all get off?

Grace (*sitting up*) No, you can't! None of you can – ow – (*wincing*) – get off! Ow! (*She lies back*)

Gorman Afraid not, ladies, this is a private stop only. This gentleman's the only one going ashore, I'm afraid. We have to make exceptions for senior management.

Inez (*impressed*) Oh!

Zandy (*equally impressed*) Oh!

Grace (*to Titus*) I warn you, you come any closer, I am summoning security.

Grace clambers up so she's now standing on the bed. Titus continues to advance, speaking simultaneously with the last.

Titus (*reassuringly*) Grace . . .

Grace (*aggressively*) I warn you! I'm warning you!

Titus Darling . . .

Grace Get away! Ow – off!

Titus Grace, darling! Gracious, it's me! It's Tim!

Grace Tim?

Titus It's Tim. Don't you know me?

Grace Tim?

Titus Yes.

Grace You're not Tim.

Titus It's me, Gracious.

Grace You look like him. A bit. Who are you? Tim's father?

Titus (*smiling*) No. I'm not my dad, Precious. I thought you might jump to that conclusion . . .

Gorman Alright if we move on, Mr Titus?

Titus Yes, thank you, Gorman.

Grace Who are you?

Gorman Thirty minutes from now, Mr Titus?

Grace Do you hear me, who are you?

Titus Thirty minutes from now, thank you, Gorman.

Grace I demand to know what's going on!

Gorman Alright, ladies? Ready to proceed, are we?

Grace What the – ow! – (*wincing again*) – is happening here? Help, somebody, help!

Inez Will you be alright, dear?

Grace Where are you going? Don't leave me here with this – ow!

Zandy She'll be alright, will she?

Gorman Don't worry, ladies, she'll be safe enough with our managing director. Alright, ladies, brace yourselves now for the next leg of our Time Leap Tour. We'll be leaping back this time one hundred and fifty years . . .

Grace Where are you all going . . . ?

Gorman If you thought times were bad now, just wait till you see this, folks . . .

Inez
Zandy } Whooo!

Grace Don't leave me alone with him . . .

Gorman (*closing the portal, muffled*) Nice to have met you, Miss. See you shortly, Mr Titus!

Inez (*muffled*) Bye!

Zandy (*muffled*) Bye!

They both give another scream as they dematerialise with Gorman in an equivalent whoosh.
Grace continues to stare at Titus with hostility.

Titus Ah! Alone at last.

Grace You come within ten centimetres of me . . . I can easily . . . I only have to . . . all I have to do is to . . .

Titus . . . is to summon your auto-butler, Adolf. Who'll come rushing in to rescue you, providing he can ever find his way, poor old thing. If I recall correctly, you'll be replacing him the moment your mother gets home . . .

Grace Who are you?

Titus Still throwing drinks in your swimming pool, is he . . . ?

Grace You – you – (*Wincing with discomfort*) Ow – ow! (*Tapping her head, angrily*) Ow-ow-ow!

Titus I see you're still fitted with the moderator.

Grace (*clasping her head*) Wretched thing – ow – it! It's unnatural. A person's got to swear occasionally, haven't they?

Titus You've only yourself to blame. That was no way to talk to your mother, was it? Calling her a – really. A girl of ten ought to know better.

Grace I was perfectly within my – how do you know that? That I called her a – ow?!

Titus If it's any consolation, in five years' time IVMs are banned. Internal Verbal Modification Treatment will be classified as an infringement of personal rights.

Grace Who are you?

Titus I'm Tim.

Grace Will you stop saying that! You are not Tim.

Titus I was when I woke up this morning.

Grace Ah-ha! Then why did he call you Titus, just now? That man?

Titus Because that's my real name. Ah-ha! I never got round to telling you, Gracious. How long have we known each other? Three weeks?

Grace Ten seconds. We've known each other for ten seconds. And stop calling me Gracious. Only Tim's allowed to call me . . . You're not Tim.

Titus No, but I will be . . .

Grace What?

Titus When I become . . . when he becomes . . .

Grace What? Becomes what?

Titus When he becomes me.

Grace (*impatiently*) What are you talking about?

Titus When he . . . when he gets to my age – when he owns half of – (*Gesturing behind him*) – that lot.

Grace Half of what lot?

Titus TLT. He's the co-founder of Time Leap Tours. He will be. When he becomes me, he will be.

Grace (*making to move towards the door*) You're mad. I'm going to call someone –

Titus No wait, wait, wait! I'm sorry.

Grace stops.

I'm telling this all wrong. I'm starting at the wrong end, I'm sorry. Would you sit down and listen to me? Just for a moment, please? Please? One minute. (*A pause*) Please.

Grace (*after a pause, reluctantly*) Alright. One minute.

Titus Maybe two.

Grace One!

Titus I'd better start from the beginning.

Grace (*sitting, deciding to humour him*) Why not?

Titus I hadn't really thought this through properly, you know. Silly of me . . .

Grace Terribly silly of you . . .

Titus It seemed so straightforward this morning. Stupid. I didn't realise it was . . . it was going to be . . . quite so . . . I should have – thought.

Grace Always good to get your story straight first . . .

Titus Right. To begin with. Fitzroy – you remember Fitzroy?

Grace Never heard of him.

Titus Fitzroy? Fitzroy Martin?

Grace I don't know any Fitzroy Martin.

Titus (*puzzled*) Strange . . .

Grace Alright? Finished? Done? (*Making to rise*) Is that it? Bye! Bye!

Titus Ah, no. Of course, you knew him as Fizz. In the old days you knew him as Fizz. Hasn't been called that for forty years. You remember Fizz . . . ?

Grace Fizz? You mean Tim's friend? Of course I remember him, I saw him yesterday with Tim. The two of them are practically never apart. Except for – now and then . . .

Titus (*smiling*) Except for now and then.

Grace What?

Titus Never mind . . .

Grace (*glaring at him*) You've got thirty seconds left. Then I'm calling someone in here and if necessary I'll ask them to throw you out of that window.

Titus Yes, you see, the point is that Fizz came good. He did it, you see. I – managed to raise the money and Fitzroy – Fizz – did the rest. With a little help from a few others. He made the brilliant breakthrough. He finally made it possible, you see.

Grace Possible to what?

Titus Possible to time travel.

Grace (*staring at him*) You are mad. You are a complete and utter – ow! –

Titus It took them years of trial and error, him and the team, but they finally did it. They cracked it.

Grace Time travel?

Titus It's amazing.

Grace It's impossible. Time travel's impossible.

Titus They said that about a lot of things.

Grace It's been proved.

Titus Here I am. Living proof.

Grace I haven't believed a single word you've said since you arrived here. In that – in that thing . . .

Titus In that what? Do you remember? It just sort of appeared, didn't it?

Grace is silent.

Where did it come from? Where did I come from, then? Through that wall? Through that solid wall?

Grace Yes . . . well . . . it could be some new . . . technology . . . or other. For – I don't know – for burglars. I mean, it's not time travel . . . that's ridiculous!

A silence.

It's merely something that can dissolve and – *merge* through . . . *blend* into other things . . . I mean, I'm not a scientist, am I? I don't know, do I?

A silence.

I mean, there's got to be some logical explanation. There must be . . .

A silence.

Other than time travel . . . that's ridiculous. Mad!

A silence. Titus waits patiently, Grace has exhausted her options.

That's really what that was just now? A time machine?

Titus A Bubble. We call it a Bubble. Not visible to the naked eye. That was a – commercial tour. The commercial wing of our company. TLT. Time Leap Tours.

Grace Time Leap Tours? Who thought that up?

Titus (*modestly*) I think it was me, actually.

Grace You could have come up with something better than Time Leap Tours, surely? Pathetic.

Titus (*a trifle hurt*) Well, it seems to have caught on with the public. We're really quite popular. These tours are definitely catching on.

Grace They don't seem that popular. There were only four people on it . . .

Titus Three, actually. One of them was the official guide.

Grace Oh, I see. The guide? In case they get lost?

Titus That sort of thing. And of course he's there to operate the . . .

Grace The Bubble? It seems rather a lot of effort for three people, doesn't it?

Titus Well, they're very pricey those trips, you know – not everyone can . . . And – we're restricted as to how many we can take at one time. There appears to be a weight limit. We had a problem early on with a school party getting trapped in the Bronze Age . . . Cost a fortune rescuing them. Ferrying them back, three at a time. Not that they were in any danger, you understand.

They were perfectly safe in their own Bubble. I mean, they weren't running round loose, you know.

Grace I'm relieved to hear it. Get eaten by a dinosaur.

Titus Oh, no. Can't have people interacting with prehistory, can you?

Grace Whatever next?

Titus Especially not schoolkids . . .

Grace Quite.

Titus Step on an insect, there's a chance you could change everything. Anyway . . .

Grace And you say Tim came up with the money to finance all this?

Titus Yes, I – A great deal of money, as a matter of fact.

Grace Tim doesn't have any money.

Titus He – managed to raise it.

Grace How could he? It must have cost a fortune.

Titus Look – currently Tim's working as a labourer. Right?

Grace Yes. You've obviously been listening to my –

Titus In about half an hour from now, as a result of a phone call from Fizz, he will leave the site, go home, get changed and then go and meet up with Fizz at the Pelican Café in Trencher Street. Which is immediately opposite the offices of the lawyers, Garbett Downside.

Grace My family's lawyers –

Titus Yes. So we found out later. But neither Fizz nor I knew that, not at the time. We had – we have an appointment at noon with Lorraine Groomfeldt –

Grace The person we usually deal with –

Titus Right. Again, we didn't know that. All we knew was this Ms Groomfeldt – telling Fizz she had a client who might possibly be interested in financing us . . . As a result of all our lobbying, we'd finally got a bite.

Grace (*suddenly more interested*) I see. And? Go on.

Titus We had the meeting – rather we *will* have this meeting with her – at twelve p.m. in – well, it's less than an hour's time from now – and, well, to put it mildly, the offer she put on the table was more than we could have dreamt of – I mean, Fizz even managed to get her to up it a bit more . . . I was . . . I was – speechless . . . but Fizz was so confident . . . as always –

Grace And who was – who is the client? Did you find that out?

Titus Yes. We did. Eventually. Once the offer was there on the table, there for the taking, it was then made clear to us that the money also came with – strings attached . . .

Grace It was from my father, wasn't it?

Titus Right. In return I had to –

Grace – you had to stop seeing me?

Titus Yes. Go away, you know. Get lost.

A pause.

Grace Although this makes absolutely no sense at all, it's beginning to sound horribly true.

Pause.

Then what happened?

He is silent. She stares at him.

They accepted the offer? Yes. You sold us out, didn't you? My God, you are Tim, aren't you? You really are Tim?

Titus (*softly*) I tried, Gracious, I really did. I'm sorry. Fizz was so excited, and she – this woman – was so – persistent – they both kept on at me . . . I couldn't see another way, not at the time . . . I thought eventually we'd, you and I, you know, we'd . . .

Grace continues to sit, digesting all this.

Of course, you kept on calling me for months afterwards – I never answered – I couldn't – You must have wondered what the hell I was . . . Listen, I came back to say I'm sorry. Fifty years later and I'm so terribly sorry. It's a decision I've had fifty years to live with and regret.

A pause. Grace moves away from him, gathering her thoughts.

Grace You've come back to apologise to me?

Titus Partly.

Grace To apologise for something which hasn't even happened to me yet?

Titus It will do, I promise. In just over an hour's time.

Grace Let me get this right. If it hasn't yet happened to me, if it's yet to happen to us . . . then I ought to be able to change it. Right?

Titus Well, in theory. It's never that simple, though. Once you change one thing, then – inevitably a whole load of other things change as well. Some for the better. A lot possibly for the worse . . .

Grace When's this meeting? What time?

Titus Twelve noon today.

Grace And the time now?

Titus (*consulting his watch*) Just after twenty past eleven. This watch may be a bit fast . . .

Grace I've still got time to call him, then, haven't I?

Titus Wait!

Grace If you're telling the truth I can warn Tim not to accept this offer. Even if you're making it up, what have I got to lose? No such meeting will even have been arranged, will it . . .?

Titus . . . oh, there's a meeting alright . . .

Grace . . . and things will carry on as normal, in that case.

Titus But what if you talk to him and they still go ahead and accept the offer?

Grace (*confidently*) He won't. Not once I've talked to him.

Titus What makes you so certain?

Grace Because I love him and Tim knows I do. If you're him, as you claim to be, you'll know I do, too.

Titus (*staring at her*) Yes, I know you do.

Grace (*staring at him*) I'd better make the call.

Silence.

Titus Listen, if I – he turns down this offer –

Grace – assuming there even is an offer –

Titus – if we turn it down, then we won't – your father won't give us the money. Which means Fizz won't be able to start the research, which means he won't have made the breakthrough. Which means we won't have started the company together. Which means I probably won't even be here. Which means, I won't have come back for you . . .

Grace Well, all that's theoretical, surely. We don't actually know whether –

She breaks off, registering what he has just said.

What do you mean, you won't have come back for me? What do you mean by that?

Titus I still love you, Gracious. As much as I ever did. I've stayed faithful to you for fifty years. What more can I say?

Grace Fifty years?

Titus I swear.

Grace What, *completely* faithful?

Titus Completely. In my mind.

Grace I see. So what are you suggesting? That I come back with you?

Titus Come forward with me, yes.

Grace Forward fifty years?

Titus Give or take a few days.

Grace That'll make me sixty-six –

Titus No, it won't –

Grace – I'll have lost fifty years of my life!

Titus No, you'll still be the same age as you are now, Gracious. Only the date will be different. You'll still be the same age.

Grace Yes, but – if I come with you – what's going to happen to the me here? If I leave the me here behind and go forward fifty years with you – what's going to happen to the me here? The rest of me? Do you see?

Titus No, you're not leaving anyone behind, Gracious. You'll be taking you with you. All of you. All of you that's existed up to now.

Grace I'll still be sixteen?

Titus Right.

Grace How old will you be?

Titus Currently? I'm sixty-eight. I'll be sixty-nine next birthday.

Grace Then, if you go forward fifty years that'll make you a hundred and eighteen?

Titus No, don't worry, I'll still be sixty-eight. Same age I am now.

Grace looks a little doubtful.

I know I don't look it, but . . . I mean, with life expectancy even in these days . . . but, in those days, believe me, the prospects are even better . . . In fifty years they've made fantastic advances . . . It's amazing . . .

A silence.

I'm in pretty good shape, you know . . . I work out regularly . . .

A silence.

(*Lamely*) You don't really want to risk it, do you?

Grace Yes, well . . . If you don't mind, I'll – I think I'll stay here and take my chances . . . I mean, I don't want to be . . . Let's face it, we'll have nothing in common, will we? Nothing to share. All the things you'd experienced in your lifetime, I'll have missed out on . . . and the things

I remember now, they'll be so long ago for you, you'll have probably forgotten all about them . . . so we wouldn't have that much to talk about really, would we?

Titus Ah, no, now wait . . .

The whooshing sound again and Gorman appears.

(*Mouthing and miming to Gorman through the closed Bubble*) Just a minute, Gorman . . . Give us a minute, will you?

Gorman acknowledges silently and then discreetly busies himself inside the Bubble.

(*A shade urgently*) Listen, Gracious, don't you see, this is a chance for us to start again. I've got plenty of money. Then.

Grace I've got plenty of money now.

Titus We could maybe take up something together . . . You know, hobbies . . . outdoor hobbies, I know you enjoy outdoors . . .

Grace You mean, going for walks together?

Titus No, I was thinking of something more like – rock climbing, you know.

Grace (*uncertain*) Rock climbing?

Titus No, what the hell! Mountaineering, let's go the whole hog, why not? Martian mountaineering. Have you ever done that? It's sensational, all those magnificent red – rocks . . . And as for that sky –

Grace No, I'm sorry, I couldn't, I'm not climbing Martian mountains with a seventy-year-old man. I couldn't. I'd just be – permanently worried about you. It's not going to work, Tim. Titus. Whatever your name is. Listen, I must make this call to Tim.

Titus Well, just you remember, that call could change it all. My life could well change.

Grace (*confidently smiling*) It certainly will. If I have my way, in fifty years, you'll have me with you for one thing. We'll be roughly the same age. Climbing mountains together –

Titus (*anxiously*) But don't you see, if things change, I might just be – you know – ordinary . . . same as everyone else . . .

Grace You won't be ordinary, I promise you that. You'll never be ordinary. Not while you have me.

Titus Yes.

Grace See you in fifty years, then.

Titus Hopefully.

Grace Definitely.

Titus I love you, Gracious. Always have done.

He signals to Gorman that he is ready to depart.

Grace Yes. Love you, too, Gorgeous. Always will do.

Gorman opens the portal. Titus steps in beside him.

Titus (*as he does so*) Did you deliver the ladies back safely, Gorman?

Gorman Ladies? (*Recalling*) Oh, those two! Yes, sir, over a week ago. They got back safely. Hold on tight, sir, please.

Gorman closes the portal. Titus waves another silent goodbye through the Bubble. Grace waves back and watches them go.

Another swoosh as Titus and Gorman apparently dematerialise.

Grace Locate Tim, please.

A beep.
Sounds of a café background.

Tim (*his voice*) Hallo, Gracious, can't talk for long, darling, we're on the way to this important meeting . . .

Grace Tim, I have to talk to you . . .

Tim (*his voice*) Yes, I'm saying we're just on our way to this –

Grace Where are you? Are you at the Pelican?

Tim (*his voice*) Yes, how did you know – ?

Grace Wait there! I'm coming over. Whatever you do, don't move!

Tim (*his voice*) Precious, we're going to be very late for this –

Grace Wait! Disconnect, please!

A beep.
The sounds cut off.

I need transport immediately! Please!

Another beep.

(*As she hurries to the door*) What's the time? Please!

Voice Eleven forty-eight and twenty-seven seconds.

Grace Thank you! (*As she goes*) I'm never going to make it!

Grace hurries out. The room is empty.
A beat later there is another swoosh and Gorman reappears as before. He has a new uniform jacket, markedly different from his TLT one, with the HEA logo (Historic Exploration Adventures). His only

passenger is Titus, who has undergone a change of image, too. Less elegant, slightly crumpled, he appears less confident and successful than previously. He is careworn and anxious.

Gorman (*opening the portal*)Here we are, Titus, back again!

Titus Thank you.

Titus disembarks immediately. There is a sense of urgency about him. He heads straight for the door.

Gorman (*calling, as Titus does so*) Better luck this time.

Titus (*as he leaves the room*) Thank you, Gorman.

Gorman I'll just hang on here for you. No hurry . . .

Titus has gone out.
Slight pause.

(*To himself*) Nice room this. Well decorated. Nice wallpaper. The wife'd like this. Knowing my luck, by my day, it'll have been discontinued.

He waits. Titus returns, disappointed.

No luck, then?

Titus No, too late.

He goes to the window and looks out.

She's left again. She's only just left.

Gorman Trouble is, the timing needs to be exact, Titus. Has to be within seconds, you know. We can never be that accurate, you see, not with these machines . . .

Titus (*not fully listening*) Yes. Quite . . .

Gorman I mean, personally, I can judge it, you know, quite accurately, within hours. Even half-hours. But seconds . . . That's asking. I mean, don't get me wrong,

I can judge a window, you know, a temporal window, as good as the next man . . .

Titus I'll just check in here – she might be in the . . .

Titus goes into the bathroom, briefly.

Gorman Yes, you do that, Titus. Just a chance she's in there, isn't there? (*Shouting through the door to Titus in the bathroom*) No, of course, every time we make this trip, Titus, your window closes that bit more, you see. The natural law being, of course, you can never land at exactly the same time twice. Limits your opportunities, doesn't it?

Titus re-enters.

You see, we can't keep doing this indefinitely . . .

Titus It's alright, I'll see you're taken care of . . . that you're alright.

Gorman No, no, that's not the problem. The point is, sooner or later, we'll start to bounce.

Titus Bounce?

Gorman We'll get bounced back. End up landing on ourselves, if we're not careful. Then we're bound to bounce. Can't be in the same place twice, can we?

Titus Oh, that. I really appreciate your help, Gorman. I hope I've made that –

Gorman No, that's quite alright, Titus. Anything for you, mate.

Titus, still abstracted, lingers in the room a little longer.

Ready to return then, are you?

Titus (*with a last look round*) Yes . . . Yes, she's long gone now . . .

Titus returns to join Gorman in the Bubble.

Gorman You know something, Titus, these little trips of yours, you've never once told me what they're all about, you know.

Titus (*reluctantly*) Well . . .

Gorman All these times we've been making them, I've been dying to ask, you know. Never liked to ask before.

Titus It's just – I'm hoping to meet up with my future wife, that's all . . .

Gorman (*touched*) Aaah! That's very romantic, Titus. That's dead romantic, mate!

Titus No, the point is, I need to warn her that she's about to make a terrible mistake. I need to warn her in time . . .

Gorman (*mystified*) Oh, I see. Hold tight, then, mate.

Gorman closes the portal. With a final swoosh they are gone.

The lights fade to a blackout.

Two

THE SURPRISE BIRTHDAY

Sometime soon. The same day.

Lorraine's office at Garbett Downside. She is a successful lawyer and her office reflects this in a tasteful, practical, unostentatious way.

A large uncluttered desk. A swivel chair. Both facing the main door, leading to the outer office occupied by her secretary, Sylvia.

In one corner a full scale Hipro – 3D holographic projector – capable of projecting full-scale images of selected callers.

The rest of the latest technology (there's a lot of it, too) is fashionably invisible, represented by a discreet keypad set into the surface of the desk.

Sylvia, a harassed thirty-year-old woman, enters. She is talking to Franklin on the overhead hands-free vocal phone.

Sylvia (*as she enters, flustered*) . . . I'm afraid I have no idea where she is, Mr Desanto . . . as I say, Ms Groomfeldt is usually at her desk by . . .

She places a hand-pad (not dissimilar to an old-fashioned iPad) with a list of Lorraine's appointments for the day on the desk.

She's invariably at her desk long before now . . . I've no idea where she is . . . I'm so sorry, Mr Desanto, I really am . . .

Franklin (*his voice*) . . . I made this appointment two days ago, Sylvia. I said I'd call Lorraine first thing this morning . . .

Sylvia (*distraught*) . . . yes, I recall you did, Mr Desanto. I distinctly entered it on her hand-pad . . .

Sylvia, after a final glance around, leaves the room again. The moment she is back in her own office, Franklin's voice also transfers automatically out there. Sylvia is speaking on auto-follow.

(*As she goes*) . . . it's down there . . . she also has a copy at home . . .

Franklin (*his voice, off*) . . . this is a matter of urgency, Sylvia. You have Ms Groomfeldt call me the minute she comes in –

Sylvia (*off*) Yes, Mr Desanto. I certainly will, Mr Desanto.

Franklin (*his voice off*) – and tell her, I expect my lawyer to be ready to take my calls at all times, day or night.

A beep from offstage as Franklin disconnects.

Sylvia (*off*) Yes, Mr Desanto, I'll be sure to tell Ms Groomfeldt that . . .

Sylvia returns with a small vase in which is a single rose. There is a card attached to the vase.

(*To herself*) I can't tell Ms Groomfeldt that. How could I possibly say that to Ms Groomfeldt . . .? I couldn't possibly.

She places the vase on the empty desk. After one or two choices of position, she feels she has it right. Lorraine is very particular.

Sylvia steps back to check things and at that moment Jan, the sixtieth-floor android janitor, enters behind her. He carries a large bunch of flowers. There is little outward sign in either his manner or speech that he is anything other than human.

Jan (*cheerfully*) Good morning, Sylvia.

Sylvia (*startled*) Oh! Good morning, Jan. Sorry I – Lovely day again.

Jan Lovely day. (*Once triggered, he goes through his programming*) Eighteen degrees, mid-town. Ten per cent above average for the time of year. With a less than five per cent probability of precipitation by mid-afternoon. Over the next twenty-four hours, it will remain clear –

Sylvia Yes, I'm sorry, Jan, I'd love to stay and small-talk but – I have . . .

Jan I'm sorry. I shall switch from small-talk mode.

Sylvia I'm sorry, normally I love to hear your forecasts in full, you know that, Jan. It's just I'm . . . I'm a trifle worried about Ms Groomfeldt. She's very late. For her. Nearly half an hour.

Jan Twenty-six minutes and fourteen seconds, yes . . .

Sylvia It's very unlike her. I hope nothing's . . .

Jan Would you like me to ascertain, Sylvia, whether she's arrived in the building?

Sylvia Oh, yes, please, would you?

Jan My pleasure, Sylvia.

A brief pause as Jan transmits and stands silently listening.

Security tell me Ms Groomfeldt has just arrived in the foyer. She is on her way up.

Sylvia Oh, thank goodness, I thought for one dreadful minute she'd – (*Noticing Jan's flowers*) What have you got there?

Jan A small token.

Sylvia Oh! How lovely! For me?

Jan No. For Ms Groomfeldt.

Sylvia Ms Groomfeldt? You're going to give those to Ms Groomfeldt?

Jan From our staff records I noted today is her birthday.

Sylvia Oh, yes, indeed it is . . .

Jan An important birthday, too. A big birthday.

Sylvia Yes, well, I wouldn't – I wouldn't mention the big bit.

Jan No? Does she not wish to celebrate that she's now sixty years of age?

Sylvia She probably won't wish to be reminded of it, Jan, not today.

Jan Curious. I should not have arranged the special greeting for her, perhaps?

Sylvia Special greeting? What special –?

Before she can continue, there is a shout of fury from the approaching Lorraine.

Lorraine (*off, approaching with a yell*) What the hell's going on in this bloody building this morning? Sylvia! SYLVIA!!

Sylvia (*alarmed*) Oh!

Jan (*calmly, smiling*) Ah, here comes the birthday girl!

Lorraine bursts into the room. She is a chic sixty and looks good. At present she is in one of her rages.

Lorraine (*as she enters*) SYLVIA! What the hell's going on? What's going on in this building this morning? Was that your doing?

Sylvia Going on, Ms Groomfeldt? I'm sorry, I –

Lorraine Every security android down there in the foyer . . . 'Happy sixtieth birthday, Ms Groomfeldt!' Did you arrange that?

Sylvia Oh, goodness, no, I –

Lorraine A bloody great ten-metre banner hanging over reception –

Sylvia Oh dear . . .

Lorraine Back there in the corridor, three of the auto-cleaners even started singing at me . . .

Jan An unfortunate misunderstanding –

Lorraine (*seeing Jan*) What's he doing here? (*Savagely*) What are you doing here?

Jan (*holding out the flowers, singing*) Happy birthday to you . . .

Lorraine (*bellowing*) GET OUT!!

Jan goes out still holding his flowers.

Jan (*as he leaves*) Switching from small-talk . . .

Lorraine attempts to calm down, standing, taking deep breaths.

Lorraine That's all I needed this morning . . . that's all I needed . . . Was that anything to do with you, Sylvia?

Sylvia Me?

Lorraine Because if it was, I promise you, you're fired. Was that you?

Sylvia No.

Lorraine Then who told them? Who?

Sylvia Lorraine, it's on file.

Lorraine What file?

Sylvia On the Central Computer. Everyone's age is on file. Every employee.

Lorraine Then have mine taken off immediately, do you hear?

Sylvia Well, I'll try – I mean –

Lorraine (*sitting*) That's all I needed today . . . Androids singing at me . . .

Sylvia Lorraine, Mr Desanto's awaiting your call.

Lorraine Call?

Sylvia You promised you'd take his call first thing this morning . . .

Lorraine Oh, my God . . . get him on! Get him on at once!

Sylvia (*leaving*) Yes, of course. Voice?

Lorraine Yes. No, visual. Whatever. Whatever he wants. Doesn't matter! Whichever! (*Seeing the vase with the rose*) Sylvia!

Sylvia (*returning immediately*) Yes, Lorraine.

Lorraine What's this – thing?

Sylvia (*meekly*) It's a – it's a small – birthday offering from me . . . just a token . . .

Lorraine Well, get rid of it! It's cluttering up the desk.

Sylvia takes up the vase, rather hurt, and goes out slowly.

(*After her*) In your own time, Sylvia. No hurry, dear!

Lorraine consults the hand-pad on her desk.

(*Scowling as she reads it*) Oh, God . . .

There is a beep and Franklin is projected on the Hipro. To all intents standing in the corner of the room. He is in his dressing gown and has a mug in his hand. He is evidently in the throes of finishing his breakfast. The birds in his garden presumably sing somewhat incongruously in the background.

Franklin Lorraine, good afternoon. Or in your case, good morning.

Lorraine (*all charm*) Franklin. I'm so sorry . . . I had this last-minute breakfast meeting and . . .

Franklin Just a minute –

He reaches out and cuts the birdsong which ceases abruptly.

That's better. I'm at the age when I'm starting to miss live birdsong. We need to get moving on this, Lorraine. I'm now getting pressure from Martha . . .

Lorraine Of course. What can I do to help?

Franklin I want you to call both those boys for a meeting. Preferably today.

His voice and image momentarily distort as the Hipro experiences a blip. What Franklin in fact says is 'This is a matter of high priority, Lorraine.'

Lorraine slaps the control panel irritably as this happens.

Push the mysterious-client angle. My name must be kept out of it till the last minute. Hold up the deal to them but hide the strings. You follow?

Lorraine You want me to see both of them?

Franklin I think that's preferable.

Lorraine (*consulting her pad*) Er – Fitzroy – Martin . . .

Franklin Fizz. He only answers to Fizz, apparently.

Lorraine Fizz? How does he spell that?

Franklin I don't know. However you usually spell Fizz.

Lorraine (*typing on her pad*) Fizz – Martin. And the other one, Tim – Armitage? Is that right?

Franklin That's the lover boy. Listen, Lorraine, I want you to fix this meeting for today, ready to roll. So all we need to do is press the button, right? I'm going upstairs now to have a final word with my little princess, try to talk her out of it.

Lorraine Save you a deal of money if you could . . .

Franklin Some chance. Grace is altogether too much like her mother. You still have those boys' contacts?

Lorraine We have them. I'll wait to hear from you.

Franklin Call you back in an hour.

Lorraine I'll be waiting, Franklin.

Franklin (*a gentle warning*) Lorraine – this time make sure you are.

Lorraine I'll be here, Franklin.

She stabs a button on the desk console.
Franklin is gone.
Lorraine pulls a face after him. She presses another button. There is a beep.

(*Addressing the ceiling mic*) Sylvia.

Sylvia (*her voice*) Yes, Lorraine.

Lorraine I'm expecting another call from Mr Desanto in an hour. Whatever I'm doing, wherever I am, put him through to me immediately.

Sylvia (*her voice*) Yes, Lorraine.

Lorraine And bring me some caffsub.

Sylvia (*her voice*) Yes, Lorraine.

Lorraine And Sylvia – connect me to – I don't know which one . . . (*She consults her pad*) . . . Fizz Martin, maybe . . .

Sylvia (*her voice*) I'm sorry, who?

Lorraine Fitzroy Martin. He's known as Fizz, apparently.

Sylvia (*her voice*) Sorry, Lorraine, how do you spell Fizz?

Lorraine I don't know. However you usually spell Fizz. Just get him, Sylvia.

Sylvia (*her voice*) Yes, Lorraine.

Lorraine is suddenly very weary. She sinks her head in her hands as if a late night has suddenly caught up with her.

Lorraine (*with a groan*) Oh, God . . .

Sylvia's voice comes back over the speaker, bringing Lorraine out of her reverie.

Sylvia (*her voice*) I'm sorry, Lorraine, I'm getting an NSR signal from Mr Martin.

Lorraine Would you speak in English please, Sylvia. What the hell's an NSR?

Sylvia (*her voice*) A non-sensory response.

Lorraine What does that mean? He's dead?

Sylvia (*her voice, with a nervous giggle*) I hope not . . . It usually means he's either sleeping deeply or he's unconscious . . .

Lorraine What's he doing sleeping? When the rest of us are wide awake? It's nine o'clock in the morning!

Sylvia (*her voice*) Oh, just a minute, there's a response now, I'm getting a response . . . Hallo? . . . Mr Martin?

Fizz (*his voice, blearily from sleep*) This is Fizz, state your biz.

Sylvia (*her voice*) Is this Mr Fitzroy Martin?

Fizz (*his voice*) Who?

Lorraine (*smoothly*) Good morning, Fizz – it's alright, Sylvia – I'll take it from here – Good morning, am I speaking to Fizz?

Fizz (*his voice*) Who is this?

Lorraine My name is Lorraine Groomfeldt, I'm a lawyer, Fizz – may I call you Fizz, by the way?

Fizz (*his voice*) A lawyer? Do I owe you money?

Lorraine (*laughing*) Not as far as I know, you don't. No, the point is I have a client – whose name I'm not at liberty to reveal – who chanced to read the proposal posted by you and your partner. And to put it briefly, Fizz, my client is extremely interested in taking things a little further. In possibly becoming involved with your project.

A silence.

Hallo. Are you still there? Fizz? Hallo . . .?

Fizz (*his voice*) Is this a joke?

Lorraine No, it's not a joke, Mr Martin, I promise you. My client would like to meet with you and your partner to discuss things further.

Fizz (*his voice*) Let's get this straight. Your client wants to invest?

Lorraine Very possibly.

Fizz (*his voice*) In our proposal?

Lorraine Yes.

Fizz (*his voice*) With money?

Lorraine I understand you were looking for investment to further your research?

Fizz (*his voice*) How much money are we talking about? I mean, this isn't going to come cheap, you know . . .

Lorraine I assure you, provided that my client is satisfied, there will be more than enough money available for your purposes, Fizz –

Fizz (*his voice*) Who is this client?

Lorraine I'm afraid I'm unable to reveal their name at present, till they're satisfied yours is a bona-fide proposal. If you and your partner would care to meet, all will be revealed . . .

Fizz (*his voice*) Meet? Where?

Lorraine May I suggest our offices, here at Garbett Downside. One-oh-eight Trencher Street. Sixtieth floor. Have you got that?

Fizz (*his voice, trying to conceal his excitement*) Yes, yes . . . sixtieth floor . . . yes. When? Exactly?

Lorraine We were hoping sometime today.

Fizz (*his voice*) Today? Well, I'll need to contact my partner.

Lorraine Yes, of course . . .

Fizz (*his voice*) He may have trouble making today. He's working, you see.

Lorraine If it turns out you can't manage it, I'll inform my client. I'm sure they'll be deeply disappointed . . .

Fizz (*his voice*) No, no, no! I could always come alone if Tim can't –

Lorraine No, it's important you're both here, Mr Martin. We need to meet both of you to confirm you're both agreeable to the offer. My client insists on that. We don't want any second thoughts or backtracking later, do we?

Fizz (*his voice*) No, of course not.

Lorraine May I get back to you then, to confirm a time?

Fizz (*his voice*) Yep.

Lorraine I look forward to meeting you in person, Fizz. I'm sorry to have woken you. Goodbye.

Fizz (*his voice*) Bye. (*As his voice cuts off, triumphantly*) Yee-haw!

Lorraine presses a button on the desk and disconnects the call but not before we have heard Fizz shout triumphantly to himself. A beep.

Lorraine Idle lout!

She sits deliberating for a moment. She looks at her watch.

(*Coming to a conclusion*) Get it over with . . .

She rather deliberately presses a couple more buttons. There are a couple of beeps again.

Suddenly Conrad is there on the Hipro. He is a TV celebrity stand-up chef, part-comic, known as a chefedian. He is in the studio and dressed for recording. Mostly his costume is recognisably a traditional chef's but with added comedy accoutrements. Behind him, the background noise of studio chatter. The call has caught him unawares.

Conrad (*to someone off camera*) . . . hang on, I've just got to take this, sweetheart . . . (*Turning and seeing Lorraine*) Oh, darling, hi! We're just about to go on air, I can't talk for long. What can I do for you? (*Turning to speak to someone off camera*) It's my wife . . . yes . . . I don't know . . . (*To Lorraine*) Sorry, darling, back with you now . . . We had this terrible early start this morning, you were asleep when I left, I didn't want to wake you. We're working all hours at the moment . . .

Lorraine Yes, I wanted you to know, darling, I have in my possession a recording of your late working session last night . . .

Conrad What?

Lorraine I had a professional colleague record you both, darling. We often use him. He's extremely reliable.

Conrad What are you talking about?

Lorraine I'm talking about your late-night session, you and your giggling, simpering, egg-juggling, culinary assistant . . .

Conrad What are you saying? You *recorded* us?

Lorraine Every single mouthful, darling . . .

Conrad Wait a minute! You paid someone to record us . . .? Is that what you're saying?

From off camera, a girl's voice is heard saying, 'Oh, my God! She recorded us . . .?' Conrad by reflex urgently waves her, one-handed, even further out of shot.

Lorraine Oh, she is there, good. All ready for the show, is she? Both her prime assets ready on parade, are they?

Conrad Darling, you have entirely the wrong –

Lorraine Dear husband, two pieces of advice. The next marriage you engage in, Conrad, if you want to emerge in better shape than you're about to from this one, first, never sign a pre-marital agreement without reading it *very* carefully if you want to be left with a penny of your own and secondly – *never* again make the mistake of marrying a lawyer!

Conrad My God, Lorraine – (*His voice breaking up as the Hipro has another blip*) I can't believe you went and did that . . .

Lorraine (*smiling*) Hope the programme goes well, dear. Hope your friend doesn't drop too many eggs.

She stabs the button to disconnect. Conrad's image goes.

(*Releasing her tension*) Bastard! Bastard! Bastard . . .

She sits shaking. Taking deep breaths to control herself.

Sylvia enters cautiously with a mug of caffsub.

Sylvia Alright, Lorraine?

Lorraine is silent, not trusting herself to speak.

I brought your caffsub. Sorry I was so long. The machine on this floor wasn't functioning again. I spoke to Jan. He's trying to fix it. He says it may need a part, though. There.

Sylvia places the mug on the desk, aware of Lorraine's state but unable to help.

Lorraine (*dully*) Thank you.

Sylvia (*gently*) Careful not to spill it on your keypad again, will you?

Lorraine My life is falling apart, Sylvia. You know that?

Sylvia Oh. Surely not. I mean, you of all people, Lorraine, you're so – so – together.

Lorraine (*dully*) Together?

Sylvia Cohesive. That's what I always admire about you. Everyone does. Your strength . . . your . . . I don't know . . . your –

Lorraine – my cohesion?

Sylvia I think that's the word. I'm sure it will pass. All you need . . . is rest . . . and a little . . .

Lorraine All I need, Sylvia, when it comes down to it, is a damned good cry and a cuddle.

Sylvia (*with a nervous laugh*) Oh, I can't possibly help you there, I'm afraid.

Lorraine No, Sylvia, you couldn't possibly.

Sylvia Well . . .

Sylvia tiptoes out. After a moment though she tiptoes in again.

I have some oxytacomol in my bag. I find those sometimes help . . . on these – occasions. Or maybe you'd like me to summon the medicart . . . I'm sure it's nothing serious . . . you know these buildings, there's always something going around. A few days ago, I know, I felt dreadful –

Lorraine (*gently*) Sylvia, would you mind leaving me alone, please.

Sylvia Yes, of course. I'm sure you'll feel better in a moment.

She goes.
Lorraine sips her drink. She wrinkles her nose at the taste.
A beep.

(*Her voice*) Mr Desanto, Lorraine, calling back on audio.

Lorraine presses a button on the desk.

Franklin (*his voice*) Lorraine?

Lorraine (*taking a deep breath*) Hallo, Franklin. Have you spoken to Grace?

Franklin Yes. Go ahead, please. Set it up immediately . . .

Lorraine You want me to meet with them?

Franklin (*his voice*) Yes, as soon as possible. Make the offer . . .

Lorraine The starting figure . . .?

Franklin (*his voice*) Yes . . .

Lorraine And I have your authority to go to twice that?

Franklin (*his voice*) Yes, no higher, no . . .

Lorraine That's maximum?

Franklin (*his voice*) That's maximum. I'll be along later.

A beep as he disconnects.
Lorraine presses a button on her desk.

Lorraine Sylvia.

Sylvia (*her voice*) Lorraine?

Lorraine Will you call Mr Martin – Fizz – and confirm my meeting with him and Mr Armitage for twelve o'clock.

Sylvia (*her voice*) What, this morning?

Lorraine Yes, of course this morning! Cancel anything else of mine.

Sylvia (*her voice*) Well, all you have is this –

Lorraine And Sylvia, tell him if they can't make it by then, both of them together, the offer's withdrawn.

Sylvia (*her voice*) Right. It's terribly short notice, you know . . .

Lorraine (*fiercely*) Just do it, Sylvia, please.

She presses the button again.
She sips her drink.
She gives a sudden convulsive sob.
She gets up suddenly and hurries out.

(*As she goes, to Sylvia outside*) Sylvia. I'll be in the washroom, I don't know what the hell's got into me today . . .!

The office is empty for a second, until a very worried Sylvia sticks her head round the door.

Sylvia Oh dear . . .

She moves to inspect the mug on the desk. She collects it up.
As she does this, Jan enters with his bunch of flowers.

Jan (*as he enters, starting to sing*) Happy birthday to you – (*Breaking off*) Ah!

Sylvia Ms Groomfeldt's in the washroom, Jan.

Jan Ah. (*Entering mild-joke mode*) Answering what we term a call of nature, eh?

Sylvia Yes. Possibly.

Jan Possibly? There is a doubt?

Sylvia I'm not quite certain exactly what Ms Groomfeldt's nature is just at present, Jan. I'm not sure that she does either.

Jan She is uncertain?

Sylvia Possibly.

Jan She is uncertain as to the nature of her nature?

Sylvia Yes.

Jan That is not natural.

Sylvia People can be contradictory at times, Jan, as you no doubt have observed.

Jan Indeed I have. Do you experience such contradictions, Sylvia?

Sylvia (*heartfelt*) Oh, yes. Yes, I do. I do frequently, Jan.

Jan I'm sorry, Sylvia. It must be confusing for you.

Sylvia Oh, you have no idea at all, Jan. You have no idea how confusing . . .

Sylvia is suddenly overcome with tears.

Excuse me, I think I need to visit the washroom . . .

Sylvia rushes out, still holding the mug.

Jan Ah. Another call of nature.

He stands a trifle perplexed in the middle of the room, still clutching his bunch of flowers, wondering what to do with them.

Something in the room beeps.
Jan registers this.
Another beep.

(*Looking to the door, calling*) Sylvia!

Another beep.

(*Calling*) Sylvia! There is a call!

Another beep.
Jan decides to answer it. He moves to the desk and presses the receive button.
Conrad appears on the Hipro.

Conrad (*as he appears*) Darling, now listen . . . (*Registering Jan*) Oh –

Jan I'm sorry Ms Groomfeldt is unable to take your call at present.

Conrad Who the hell are you?

Jan I am Jan Sixty. Security and maintenance supervisor sixtieth floor, number one-oh-eight Trencher Street.

Conrad You're an android?

Jan That is correct. Series twelve. Modified.

Conrad What are you doing answering Ms Groomfeldt's personal Hipro?

Jan I repeat, Ms Groomfeldt is unable to take your call at present.

Conrad Why not? Where is she?

Jan She is in the washroom. She is currently undergoing contradictions.

Conrad She's what?

Jan In her nature.

Conrad Well, tell her Conrad – her husband called.

Jan Her husband?

Further Hipro interference as Conrad says, 'Tell her I need to speak to her urgently.'

Conrad (*audible again*) No, wait – where's her secretary? Where's Sylvia? Put me on to Sylvia, then.

Jan I regret that Sylvia is experiencing confusions.

Conrad I don't believe this. Isn't there anyone there I can talk to? Would you tell me what the hell's happening there?

Jan I can only presume that it is a case of over-excitement. As a result of Ms Groomfeldt's big birthday.

A silence.

Conrad (*stunned*) Oh, my God . . . Her birthday! It's her birthday, isn't it? (*With a cry*) IT'S HER FUCKING BIRTHDAY, YOU IDIOT!

He slaps his head and stabs at an unseen button.

Jan Indeed it is! Sixty years old! Tell me, do you consider these flowers are a suitable . . .

Conrad has gone.

(*To himself*) More contradictions.

He stands, once again deliberating what to do with the flowers.

Sylvia returns, having tidied herself up a bit.

Sylvia Oh, Jan, are you still here?

Jan There was a Hipro call from Ms Groomfeldt's husband.

Sylvia (*scowling*) Really? What did he want?

Jan To speak to Ms Groomfeldt.

Sylvia I don't think she'll want to talk to him somehow.

Jan He seemed extremely upset to learn it was her birthday.

Sylvia Huh! He'd probably forgotten it.

Jan Forgotten it?

Sylvia Very probably.

Jan (*mystified*) How could he have possibly forgotten her big birthday?

Sylvia Oh. Men like – that – men like Conrad Cato – so-called celebrities – so busy with their half-baked careers – they're – how did my father put it? – lower than pond-life . . .

Jan Pond-life?

Sylvia . . . obsessed with nothing but themselves – he's totally unworthy of her, Jan . . . She's a top lawyer, for goodness' sake! And he's – what? A failed daytime stand-up chefedian. His cooking's dreadful and his jokes are dire. Ms Groomfeldt married beneath her.

Jan Beneath her?

Sylvia He treats her like – dirt – how dare he –? How *dare* he? He's not fit to be her doormat . . . She's a fine woman, Jan!

Jan Oh, yes. She is! She is, Sylvia.

Lorraine returns, more subdued.

Lorraine God, I look terrible. I don't look sixty, I look more like eighty . . .

Sylvia (*loyally*) You look wonderful, Lorraine.

Lorraine Hah!

Jan You look a million dollars.

Lorraine (*glaring at him*) What's he doing here?

Sylvia He – he was answering . . . he was just answering . . .

Jan (*another of his jokes*) A call of nature . . . (*He laughs*)

Lorraine What are you doing here?

Jan (*holding out the flowers*) From an admirer.

Lorraine Are those from whom I think they're from?

Jan Indeed they are.

Lorraine Well, take them away.

Jan Certainly. Where would you like me to put them?

Lorraine In the nearest rubbish bin.

Jan Of course.

Jan goes out, cheerfully enough.

Lorraine (*scowling after him*) That thing's overdue for a service. It's completely unhinged. What's the time? Is it time for me to meet those boys?

Sylvia A minute or two yet. I've reserved meeting room nine for you.

Lorraine When Mr Desanto arrives, show him straight up, will you? He can wait here in my office.

Sylvia He won't be joining you for the meeting?

Lorraine No, he prefers not. It's an awful lot of money, I must say. Simply to pay someone not to marry your precious daughter.

Sylvia Yes, well, even love has a price, I suppose . . .

Lorraine Cheaper to have him shot.

Sylvia (*slightly shocked*) Oh.

Lorraine Shoot both of them, come to that. She's a spoilt little brat, too. Twists her father round her little finger. She fancies being a dancer, not a single academy will accept her, so what does he do? He ends up buying her a ballet school, for God's sake. (*Impatiently*) Where are they, then? They're late.

Sylvia It's only just time. Oh, by the way, your husband called just now. I . . . Yes.

Lorraine I have been a lawyer for over thirty years, Sylvia, you know that?

Sylvia Yes, Lorraine.

Lorraine I have a fine reputation. I pride myself on rarely making a wrong choice, accepting a wrong client, taking the wrong course of action or anticipating a wrong verdict.

Sylvia Yes, Lorraine.

Lorraine But despite an almost unblemished record, do you want to know the single most glaring error of judgement I have ever made in my entire life, Sylvia?

Sylvia Your choice of husband, Lorraine. I'm so sorry.

Lorraine I want no more calls from that bastard, you hear? Block all calls, Sylvia.

Sylvia Yes, Lorraine. (*She hovers in the doorway*) Well, if there's nothing more I can . . .

Lorraine Sylvia –

Sylvia Yes?

Lorraine I apologise. You must have been through – through all this, so many . . . I apologise.

Sylvia That's alright, that's what I'm here for, Lorraine . . .

Lorraine You know, I've never asked you, Sylvia – do you have a – a relationship of any sort? I know you're not married, but – do you have any sort of partnership with anyone? Some man? Woman?

Sylvia Yes. There is someone. I'm seeing . . . now and then . . . He's – he's a –

Lorraine He's what?

Sylvia Well, he's a – he's a deep-sea diver, actually.

Lorraine Good Lord! Really?

Sylvia Which means he's away rather a lot, of course. Diving. Deep sea. You know. But we've had some wonderful holidays together. Swimming with – dolphins and so on.

Lorraine Dolphins! Lovely!

Sylvia And. Other things. Cuttlefish and things.

Lorraine (*genuinely amazed*) Good heavens! I never knew that! You never told me this before. Cuttlefish! How glamorous. How on earth did you both meet?

Before Sylvia can reply there is a beep.

Voice Mr Martin and Mr Armitage in the main foyer.

Sylvia (*moving to the door*) I'll have them shown up.

Lorraine (*moving with her*) Room nine, you say?

Sylvia (*as she goes*) Room nine. Do you need anything with you . . .?

They both go out. The room is empty again.

There is a brief pause and the Hipro beeps again. And again. Jan enters. He now has the flowers arranged incongruously in a waste bin. He arranges

this on the desk carefully, reproducing Sylvia's movements she made earlier with her own vase. The Hipro beeps a third time. He presses the console.
Conrad appears again.

Conrad Listen, darling – Oh, it's you again.

Jan I'm sorry Ms Groomfeldt is unable to take your call at present.

Conrad She can't still be in the washroom?

Jan I'm sorry Ms Groomfeldt is unable to take your call at present.

Conrad Look, has she put you up to this? Blocking my calls? I'm warning you, you'd better let me speak to her, mate. Do you know who I am?

Jan I do indeed. You're her husband.

Conrad I'm a fucking celebrity, mate.

A brief Hipro crackle.

Now put her on at once, you stupid machine –

Jan Correction. I am a model A for Adam 339-zero-7 R for Robert 68514 double zero, modified series twelve. You, on the other hand, are Conrad Cato, a failed day-time stand-up chefedian whose cooking is dreadful and whose jokes are dire. You are lower than pond-life and unfit to be your wife's doormat, Mr Cato. Good day to you.

Before Conrad can recover, Jan stabs the button.
Conrad goes.
Jan adjusts his floral arrangement. He admires it from several angles, finally sitting behind the desk in Lorraine's chair.
Franklin enters.

Franklin (*to Sylvia, offstage behind him*) . . . Thanks, Sylvia. I'll wait for her here.

Franklin sits on the sofa and makes himself comfortable.

(*Seeing Jan for the first time, startled*) My God! Who are you?

Jan I am Jan. Sixtieth Floor Security and Maintenance Supervisor. Model A for Adam 339-zero-7 R for Robert 68514 double zero, modified series twelve.

Franklin How do you do? Franklin.

Jan How do you do, Franklin. I am an android.

Franklin I gathered.

Jan You are comfortable with that?

Franklin What, with you being an android? Why not?

Jan There are many who are not. I sensed from your manner that I might have alarmed you.

Franklin No, I didn't expect to see you there. You surprised me, that's all. What were you doing? Sitting there in Ms Groomfeldt's chair?

Jan I was – ensuring the desk was safe. That it was – secure. A – routine maintenance check . . . (*He adjusts the flowers*)

Franklin (*watching him*) Were you indeed? (*A pause*) If you hadn't told me you were an android, I would have had the distinct impression that you're one hell of a liar.

Jan Indeed? (*He adjusts the flowers again*)

Franklin But since you are clearly an android and therefore incapable of lying, I'm faced with the problem that, if you are indeed lying, then maybe you were also lying about the fact that you're an android. Which would clearly be a lie because you certainly are an android and were therefore telling the truth about checking that the desk was safe. Which is patently a load of rubbish. You appreciate my dilemma, Jan whatever-your-name-is?

Jan (*after a slight pause*) True. I was lying. About the desk. I am truthfully a series twelve modified. I contain a sub-routine which permits occasional harmless falsehood.

Franklin Does it now? That's a dangerous modification to make to an android, don't you think? If you lot start lying as well, we're none of us going to know where the hell we are. We humans have got very used to androids always telling us the plain truth. What's it going to do to the human race if you start lying to us as well? Few of us humans can trust each other as it is, now we can't even trust the machines.

Jan As I say, the modification restricts us to occasional harmless falsehood.

Franklin How would you classify an occasional harmless falsehood?

Jan Harmless. One which does not cause either hurt or distress to a human. Occasional. A falsehood that is employed occasionally.

Franklin And how would you define occasionally?

Jan If used too frequently, there is an override which causes the unit to shut down entirely.

Franklin In other words, if you tell too many lies you'll drop dead?

Jan Put at its simplest.

Franklin I know a few people I've done business with who could have benefited from that modification.

Jan laughs loudly and abruptly. Franklin looks at him, rather startled.

Jan Most amusing! I also have humour. Model twelve modified also has humour.

Franklin Good God!

Jan I identified that what you said was a joke. I responded with laughter. Was I correct in doing so?

Franklin It was – it was a kind of a joke, yes.

Jan I see. I apologise if my laughter was incorrect. The humorous modification is still experimental. There is a danger of misinterpreting and laughing inappropriately. I would not want that.

Franklin I daresay someone will tell you, if you laugh inappropriately.

Jan You think so?

Franklin People – tend to be a little sensitive if they feel they're being laughed at inappropriately. (*A pause*) I like the flowers. That's an unusual arrangement. Who did they come from?

Jan (*adjusting the flowers*) I have no idea.

Franklin I sense you're occasionally lying again, Jan. Be careful, I don't want you to drop dead on me.

Jan (*swiftly*) Me. The flowers came from me. I bought them for Ms Groomfeldt's birthday.

Franklin It's Lorraine's birthday?

Jan I purchased them from the shop in the precinct.

Franklin I'm sure she was very touched.

Jan No. She was not at all. Indeed, she appeared quite angry.

Franklin Well now, you surprise me . . .

Jan There is a ninety-two per cent probability of floral gifts being appreciated by females. Especially for birthdays, anniversaries or apologies.

Franklin Maybe Lorraine's in the other eight per cent. Had you considered that?

Jan It is possible. She is unusual.

Franklin Or maybe she just didn't care for the vase.

Jan I agree. It is not elegant.

Franklin Perhaps you should change it?

Jan That is what she requested.

Franklin Really?

Jan Maybe I should have purchased her chocolates instead?

Franklin Yes, possibly. Women always like chocolates. They generally pretend not to but they eat them all the same. Boxes of them.

Jan Seventy-eight per cent of women –

Franklin Yes, Jan, I wouldn't take these percentage figures of yours too literally. Believe me, women don't break down too easily into percentages. You're talking to someone who's been around for seventy years, son, take it from me . . . Lorraine's an individual.

Jan She is.

Franklin Knowing her, you'd probably be better off buying her a good bottle of brandy.

Jan Brandy?

Franklin Five star.

Jan Brandy is only a seven per cent –

Franklin Believe me, a good brandy is a damn sight more than seven per cent.

Jan You are extremely knowledgeable, Franklin.

Franklin About brandy?

Jan About women.

Franklin (*modestly*) Well, as I say, I've been around a little.

The console beeps. Jan presses a button.
Conrad appears on the Hipro.

Conrad Hi, darling, listen I – just wanted to . . .

Jan rapidly stabs the button again.
Conrad disappears as quickly as he appeared.

Franklin (*bemused at the speed of this*) Who was that?

Jan Wrong number. This is a very fortuitous meeting. Is there any further advice you can give me, Franklin? Concerning women?

Franklin Well, it's a matter of instinct, really . . . You learn on the job, as you go . . .

Jan Yes, yes. Up until my recent modification, you understand, I never experienced these feelings. They are new and – may I say – exciting.

Franklin Yes, they can be. First time round. They can be. Listen, if I could tell you only one thing to bear in mind, it's this. If you do happen to argue – and believe me, if you spend any time in a woman's company, you're both of you almost certainly bound to argue eventually – never ever try and win. On the rare occasion that you do win, you'll almost certainly live to regret it. Women have long memories – long emotional memories . . . You understand what I'm talking about, emotional memories?

Jan (*engrossed by this masterclass*) Long emotional memories, yes.

Franklin When an argument ends, men walk away and tend to forget all about it . . . But women *remember* – they stay with it . . . Two words to bear in mind in a relationship, son . . . (*Holding up his fingers*) Concede. Gracefully.

Jan Concede. Gracefully. Yes.

Franklin Take my tip, start by getting rid of those flowers, they're never going to do the trick.

Jan picks up the flowers and starts for the door.

Jan Five star brandy, yes?

Franklin At least. I think the Greeks may even make a twelve star.

Jan (*hurrying out*) Thank you, Franklin . . .

Sylvia enters as Jan is leaving.

Sylvia Oh, Jan, where are you going with those . . .?

Jan leaves.

(*To Franklin*) He's behaving most peculiarly, he really is. Lorraine's right. I don't know what's got into him lately, I'm sure.

Franklin I think he's having trouble with his modifications, poor fellow . . .

Sylvia I don't quite understand.

Franklin I don't think he does either . . .

Sylvia No sign of Lorraine yet. I just popped in to see if you needed anything, Mr Desanto. Cup of tea? Coffee? Caffsub?

Franklin No thanks, Sylvia, I'm fine.

Lorraine enters.

Sylvia Oh, she's here.

Lorraine Well, that was illuminating . . . very illuminating . . .

Sylvia Have the gentlemen left, Lorraine?

Lorraine They were both just leaving.

Sylvia Excuse me, I'll just go and see them out, then . . .

Sylvia leaves.

Franklin How did it go? No joy, eh?

Lorraine Well, I gave it my best, Franklin. To begin with, I had the odd-looking one, Fizz, eating out of my hand . . . desperate for the money. He'd have done practically – I thought he was at one stage . . . But the other one. Your one. Tim. He wasn't going to budge. Keen enough to start with. But once I revealed the strings, as soon as he realised he was being bought off . . . All I can say is he must be either madly in love or . . .

Franklin Or believes he is . . .

Lorraine I sensed he'd been got at, you know . . . He seemed prepared. Forewarned. As though he'd already talked it over with your daughter. Only I can't see how he can have –

Franklin She's a determined girl, Grace. Usually gets what she wants. Or what she believes she wants at the time.

Lorraine Anyway, they said no. I'm sorry, Franklin, I tried my best.

Franklin Saved me a six-figure sum, anyway.

Lorraine Wait till you see my fee. Anything else you want me to do to try and stop it? Short of hiring a hit man . . .? Or locking her away in a lunar prison?

Franklin No. I think the best course now is, if you can't beat them . . .

Lorraine What? Join them?

Franklin You know I think we've both reached the age, Lorraine, when we have a responsibility to the next generation to keep one foot in the door to the future, rather than leaving it to slam in their faces. (*Moving to the door*) Thank you anyway, for trying . . . I'll be in touch. Happy birthday, by the way.

Lorraine Oh, thank you. How did you know that?

Franklin A little bird told me. A little love bird . . .

Lorraine What?

Franklin (*going out*) Talk soon.

Franklin leaves.
Lorraine stands for a moment.
She sits and examines the console. She frowns, puzzled.
Sylvia returns.

Lorraine I have had two calls, apparently, on my personal Hipro line. Both have been answered.

Sylvia Really?

Lorraine Who answered them?

Sylvia Mr Desanto, possibly?

Lorraine Franklin?

Sylvia He was the only one in here.

Lorraine Odd.

Sylvia You had a couple of calls out there on the main line as well. Both from your husband. I blocked those as you asked.

Lorraine Good. Have they gone, then? Those two young men?

Sylvia Yes. They'd obviously been having – quite an argument, both of them . . .

Lorraine I'm not surprised. They were virtually at each other's throats when I left. We've obviously broken up a beautiful friendship, there. The geeky one – Fizz, he's – rather interesting, when you meet him . . . he may have . . . I've a feeling he may turn out to be rather special . . .

Sylvia The girl was waiting in the foyer. The daughter. She and the other boy, Tim, were waiting for Mr Desanto to give them both a lift. The geeky one went off on his own . . .

Lorraine Poor boy . . .

Sylvia Yes, poor Fizz, he looked very lonely, poor thing . . .

Lorraine No, not Fizz. The other one. He's who I feel sorry for.

Sylvia Really? He's the lucky one, surely? He's found true love? What can be more romantic than that? Sacrificing everything for love?

Lorraine Oh, for God's sake, Sylvia, you great damp puddle . . .

Sylvia I almost envy them both, I really do . . .

Lorraine . . . you great wet rag of a woman! Go home. Stop covering my office in sentimental – treacle.

Sylvia You want me to close down?

Lorraine No, I'll stay on for a little. I have a bit more to do. I've done practically nothing today.

Sylvia Well, don't work too late, will you? Not on your birthday. It's a special day!

Lorraine Go and have a cold bath with your deep-sea diver!

Sylvia (*cheerfully, as she goes*) Oh! That could be fun! 'Night-night, Lorraine!

Sylvia leaves.
Lorraine starts to work on her pad.
After a moment she reaches for the keypad on her desk.
The lights dim.
Soft jazz music starts to play.
Lorraine works on.
Jan enters. He has a bottle of brandy.
Lorraine at first fails to notice him.
Jan places the bottle on the desk. She looks up.

Lorraine (*scowling at the bottle*) Is that from whom I think it's from?

Jan Indeed it is.

Lorraine Then take it away and pour it down the nearest toilet.

Jan Certainly. (*He picks up the bottle and hesitates*) I – have to tell you this was extremely expensive.

Lorraine I don't care what it cost! Throw it away!

Jan (*hesitating*) It cost in excess of sixty-five credits and, though I am well remunerated for my duties in Security and Maintenance, I can hardly afford to use this as a substitute toilet cleaner.

Lorraine waves a hand over the console and dims the music slightly which continues to play in the background.

Lorraine Wait a minute! You mean you paid for it as well? He didn't even pay for it?

Jan Who didn't even pay for it?

Lorraine (*growing angrier*) The bastard didn't even pay for it?

Jan The bastard certainly did not! I paid for it!

Lorraine In other words, he made you pay for it? He told you to go out and buy it and pay for it out of your own hard-earned money?

Jan No, no! Nobody told me to pay for it. I bought it and paid for it myself.

Lorraine You bought it for you?

Jan For me? I don't even drink.

Lorraine (*loudly*) Then what the hell did you buy it for?

Jan I bought it for you.

Lorraine *Me?* I didn't order it!

Jan I know you didn't order it.

Lorraine (*shouting*) Then what the hell did you buy it for, you idiot?

Jan (*shouting*) I bought it for you as a present, you foolish woman!

A slight pause.

We appear to be having an argument.

Lorraine What?

Jan In which case, I concede gracefully.

Lorraine (*calmer*) You spent all your money on an expensive bottle of brandy, brandy you can't even drink, and then you give it to me. Why?

Jan Because I am in love with you, Lorraine.

Lorraine, for once in her life, is speechless.

Lorraine I'm – a – I'm a . . . You're a . . . you're a . . . I'm a – (*Rather lamely*) I'm a married woman . . .

Jan I know that. Your husband is also lower than pond-life . . . and unfit to be your doormat.

Lorraine (*grabbing the bottle*) I need a drink. I'm hallucinating here! I need a glass of this.

Jan Oh dear, I have brought no glass. Shall I fetch one?

Lorraine (*wrestling with the screw top*) It doesn't matter . . . This is an emergency.

She swigs deeply from the bottle.

(*Choking slightly*) Oh, God!

Jan Is it good?

Lorraine (*her eyes watering*) It's deadly!

Jan Oh dear, I'm sorry. Shall I go out and purchase an alternative?

Lorraine No, no. This'll do! This'll do nicely.

She takes another swig.

(*Toasting him*) Down the hole!

Jan Happy birthday!

Lorraine (*hoarsely*) Thank you. It does, it tastes exactly like toilet cleaner.

Jan Be careful, it might be toxic.

Lorraine It is. It's extremely toxic. I'm getting slightly drunk, very quickly . . .

Jan Is that good?

Lorraine For me, yes. For you it could be disastrous. We shall see. Listen, I need to eat something very soon, or else I'll . . . Do you fancy going out, getting a bite to eat somewhere? Oh no – you don't eat either, do you? I was forgetting.

Jan No. But it would be a pleasure to watch you eat, Lorraine . . .

Lorraine in her emotional state finds this extremely funny. She laughs. So does Jan, though he's less sure why. They continue for a moment. They stop.

Lorraine No, no, no . . . That would be no fun. Listen, what would you like to do? I'm having all the fun here. You're not having any fun at all, are you, watching me drinking? . . . What would you like to do? You choose.

Jan (*moving closer, tentatively*) If I were offered the choice, Lorraine, I would like more than anything . . .

Lorraine No, I don't think that would be wise. Not on a first date, darling . . .

Jan Would it not be in order for us to dance?

Lorraine Dance? You just want to dance? Is that all you want to do?

Jan Yes. If you would consent.

Lorraine Oh, God. Yes. Why not? Why the hell not? Let's dance.

She and Jan start to dance together, rather self-consciously and formally to begin with.

(*After a moment*) Hold me. Hold me closer, lover . . . tightly . . . that's it. Cuddle me . . . give us a cuddle . . .

Jan draws her closer to him. They dance a little more. Lorraine starts crying softly at first, then louder and louder.

Jan Are you sad, Lorraine?

Lorraine (*still crying*) No, lover, I'm very happy . . . I've never been happier . . .

She cries on. Jan is puzzled for a moment, then assuming she is joking, he laughs.

The music builds.

She continues crying. He continues laughing.

On this somewhat contradictory scene, the lights fade to a blackout.

Three

SURPRISES

Fifty years hence. A portion of two separate offices, primarily the occupants' desks.

The first is Sylvia's outer office, now on the fifty-ninth floor of the Trencher Street building. One door leading to the corridor and the other to the inner sanctum, Mervyn Cutler's office.

The other office is Titus's, a slightly larger inner office with one door. He, like Lorraine earlier, also has a Hipro unit in one corner.

There is a third area representing a virtual bar, a small area of the 'In Your Dreams' fantasy website, so popular with couples at this time.

At present Seraphina, a glamorous exotic dancer, is lolling against the bar. Restless, bored and waiting for someone. She is, it transpires, Sylvia's avatar. Sylvia, now aged eighty, is standing in her office also leaning on her desk in a pose which emulates Seraphina's. Sylvia wears a neat slip-on 'cerebral collar', the only piece of technology to indicate she is currently connected to the 'In Your Dreams' site. Initially when Seraphina speaks it is a fraction after Sylvia has done. This is merely to establish the convention. Eventually, the avatar speaks as its principal mouths along simultaneously with it. The avatar's speech pattern, style and movement are all its own, though. The principal is only there to choose words and to dictate broad choices of movement.

Behind the bar is Bellina, a virtual barmaid and the Location Facilitator.

Soft music plays. Distant background voices are also heard, drifting in from other unseen areas of the bar.

Bellina (*bored*) He's late again, eh?

Sylvia Yes . . .

Seraphina Yeah . . .

Bellina That's men. Stir you up, set you up, stand you up.

Sylvia Not this one . . .

Seraphina Not this one . . .

Sylvia This one's worth it . . .

Seraphina This one's worth it.

Bellina That good, huh?

Sylvia (*smiling*) Oh, yes . . . (*She wriggles her hips*)

Seraphina (*smiling*) Oh, yes . . . (*She wriggles her hips*)

Bellina laughs.

Bellina Want another, while you're waiting?

Sylvia No.

Seraphina Nah.

Titus enters his office area hurriedly. He is late for their appointment. He pulls off his jacket and takes his own cerebral collar from his desk.

Titus (*breathless*) Oh, God . . .

Bellina (*as this happens*) Been working today, honey . . . ?

Sylvia Yes . . .

Seraphina Yeah.

Bellina Dancing, huh?

Sylvia Yes. A little bit of horse, little bit of pole, little bit of easel. You know . . . the usual . . .

Seraphina Yeah. A little bit of horse, little bit of pole, little bit of easel. You know . . . the usual . . .

Titus is now ready. He starts to walk on the spot in his office.

Titus Hey!

Fabiano (*mirroring Titus, as he enters the bar*) Hey!

Bellina (*seeing Fabiano*) Hey! What time is this, big man? Welcome back to *In Your Dreams*.

Fabiano enters the bar. He is a glamorous pilot, the confident captain of a space freighter.

Titus Hi!

Fabiano (*to Seraphina*) Hi!

Bellina Hey, mister, this is no way to treat a beautiful lady . . .

Sylvia Where've you been . . .?

Seraphina Where've you been?

Titus Apologies, sweetheart . . .

Fabiano Apologies, sweetheart . . .

Titus . . . ran into a little trouble . . .

Fabiano . . . ran into a little trouble . . .

Sylvia Trouble?

Seraphina Trouble?

Titus . . . quarantine issue on Lunar Base . . .

Fabiano . . . quarantine issue on Lunar Base . . .

Titus . . . we had this cargo of Venusian Marsh Puppies . . .

Fabiano . . . we had this cargo of Venusian Marsh Puppies . . .

Bellina Cute!

Titus . . . had to wait for clearance . . .

Fabiano . . . had to wait for clearance . . .

Sylvia Venusian Marsh . . .? (*Her voice begins to fade under her avatar's*)

Seraphina . . . Marsh Puppies . . .? I don't think I've ever seen one . . .

Bellina They're cute. My sister has four of them.

Titus If you're good, I promise . . . (*His voice starts to fade under*)

Fabiano . . . good, I promise to bring you one next trip to Venus.

During the next section, Sylvia and Titus mouth along with their counterparts while echoing their movement.

Seraphina (*seductively*) Good? How good do you want me to be?

Fabiano (*taking her in his arms*) Really bad.

Seraphina (*holding him*) Really bad?

Fabiano (*kissing her gently*) The worst.

Seraphina (*kissing him in turn*) The worst?

Fabiano (*kissing her*) I've wanted you so badly . . .

Seraphina (*kissing him*) That good, eh?

Fabiano (*kissing her*) I've never had it so bad . . .

Seraphina (*kissing him*) I'll make it good again, baby . . .

The two go into a prolonged kiss.

Sylvia and Titus in their separate areas embrace the air.

Bellina looks on amused.

Bellina There they go again . . .

The couple finally separate.
They both take a deep breath as they gaze into each other's eyes.

Seraphina Mmmm!

Fabiano Mmmm!

Bellina When you folks are through, room five upstairs is vacant. Do me a favour there and move it along, will you? I'm in need of the bar space.

Fabiano (*questioning*) Uh-huh?

Seraphina (*consenting*) Uh-huh.

In his office, Titus's Hipro terminal gives a beep.
Fabiano stops. Titus looks round.
Fabiano releases Seraphina.

Fabiano Oh, hell . . .

Seraphina What's wrong?

Another beep.

Fabiano I have to take this . . . I'm sorry . . .

Titus (*taking off his collar*) I'm sorry . . . Sorry . . . sorry . . . sorry . . .

Fabiano . . . sorry . . . sorry . . . sorry . . .

Fabiano exits.
Titus sits at his desk and consults his keypad.
Sylvia and Seraphina stand indignantly.

Bellina You want to wait for him, honey? Keep it warm?

Sylvia No, sod him.

Seraphina No, sod him.

Sylvia takes off her collar and exits angrily.
Seraphina exits angrily.
Bellina is left alone behind the bar.

Bellina Yeah. Good choice, girl.

The lights fade as the virtual location is disconnected. Bellina goes.
Titus meanwhile having checked the caller ID on his terminal has smartened himself up, removed his collar and now answers his Hipro.
Franklin, now quite elderly (one hundred and twenty) appears. He is on holiday by a swimming pool somewhere. He is dressed colourfully with a tropical cocktail in hand.

Titus Franklin . . .

Franklin Titus, dear boy . . .

Titus How's the holiday?

Franklin Ah, well, you know . . . when you get to my age, a holiday's a holiday . . . I've had over a hundred years of them . . . after a time, they all merge into one . . .

Titus How's Grace? Still enjoying herself up there?

Franklin Yes, she seems to be. She's in the beauty salon. Making a few low-gravitational improvements. I told her, she looks perfectly fine. But women, they won't be . . . Sends her love. Misses you a lot.

Titus Yes. I'm sure. What can I do for you, Franklin?

Franklin Just checking in to see the old firm was still there.

Titus Oh, yes. We're still here. Keeping up. Just about. I sent you through last week's figures, didn't you get them? They're good. Considering.

Franklin Yes, I got them. I got them.

A silence. Titus waits.
Franklin sips his drink.

(*Pulling a face*) Even the drinks up here are terrible. Lemons don't grow well, you know, in low gravity. They aren't happy. It does something to their skins.

Titus That a fact?

Franklin No, it's not a fact. It's just a theory of mine. Same with oranges. Same with limes. Any citrus fruit is the same . . .

Titus Yes, I'm sure. Listen, Franklin, I appreciate you haven't called me all the way from the moon just to discuss fruit. What can I do for you?

Franklin Yes. (*A pause*) Titus, I had a report that you've been taking regular time tours on the firm, is that right?

Titus Yes. I'm expected to make regular checks. As vice-chief executive, I'm required to keep an eye on things first hand, occasionally.

Franklin Does that also include making unscheduled disembarkations?

Titus I don't follow you.

Franklin You've made sixteen apparently. Over the last thirty years. All visiting the same temporal location. July ninth, fifty years ago, between approximately eleven a.m. and twelve p.m. Sixteen trips in total. All unauthorised, unscheduled disembarkations.

Titus God, have you been checking on me?

Franklin Titus, I'm still in overall charge. I'm kept informed of these things. Nobody can get away with unscheduled disembarkations, not even you, the boss's son-in-law. Nobody can. What the hell are you playing at?

Titus (*muttering*) I was trying to set things straight. That's all. With Grace.

Franklin Titus. It's happened . . . don't meddle with it. Don't monkey with the past, son. Aside from anything else, you're breaking the law. I don't have to remind you, there are strict legal penalties. Nothing good ever came from trying to alter things.

Titus But I already . . .

Franklin What? You already what?

Titus Nothing.

Franklin I seem to recall that particular July was the month you turned down my offer, wasn't it? My offer for you to take a large sum of money to leave Grace alone. But instead you went right ahead, proposed to her and married her. Against both her parents' wishes, especially her late mother's, God bless her. Face it, Titus, you turned down my offer and you chose to marry Grace. So I gave the money instead to your partner. Fitzroy came good and I now own the firm. Things all ended happily. Leave them be.

Titus For the record, I didn't propose to her, Grace proposed to me.

Franklin Listen, if you're having trouble with your marriage and trying to put it right by going back fifty years and unmarrying the girl, I have to tell you that is no decent way for a gentleman to behave, Titus. As my late grandmother used to say, you've made your bed, now lie on it, lump it and die on it. Is that clear?

Titus Then how do you suggest we do put it right, Franklin? Grace and me? You tell me that.

Franklin You've been fifty years together this year, right?

Titus Right.

Franklin Don't you think that's enough?

Titus Enough? What do you mean, 'enough'?

Franklin (*fumbling in his pocket*) Excuse me – just a minute –

Franklin takes a strip of tablets from his pocket and swallows one.

– Still have this confounded GDD . . . Listen, when I was young, I can remember even in those days people dying aged seventy – eighty years top . . . incredible to think of now. Many people then considered themselves lucky to make it even to ninety. These days, let's face it, we all live far too long – far longer than intended – look at me, I'm a hundred and twenty – I've had so many replacement parts there's practically nothing left of the original – What's more, my doctor tells me that, barring accidents or acts of God, I have at least sixty good years ahead of me. One hundred and eighty years, Titus. Now where do you think that leaves love? Delicate, fragile love? We simply weren't designed to love for that long, Titus. Especially not a man and a woman. In the old days, when you vowed to love somebody till your dying day, you used to know more or less what you were getting into. Three score years and ten, thank you ma'am, and goodnight. Some people couldn't even hold out that long. But endless, limitless love, year after year, we're talking seven score years and ten in many cases, Titus . . . for most of us, after a time, love just wears out its welcome. Titus, if you're feeling unloved, maybe it's because Grace's love for you has simply worn out. She takes after Martha in lots of ways.

Titus Did Martha stop loving you?

Franklin I think she may have done. Why else avoid coming home? Chasing around the solar system fixing air-conditioning plants. Until she finally . . . until her accident . . .

Titus And you? Did your love for her wear out, too?

Franklin (*after a pause, gazing up at the sky*) Listen, the sat's about to go dark side and we'll lose the decent signal. We'll talk again. Meanwhile, stay in your own time, do you hear me? I'll stop here moonside and keep my little girl company. Don't worry, I'll take care of her. Sixty-seven years old next birthday and I still think of her as my little girl . . . still loves her daddy, bless her. Now her mother's gone, she's all I have, Titus.

Franklin goes.

Titus Look, Franklin, will you tell Grace I'll . . .

He gives up.
He sits for a moment.
He takes up his collar, contemplating returning to the site. He hesitates but reconsiders. He puts the collar back in the drawer and leaves the office.

(*As he goes*) Oh, God . . .

As he leaves, Sylvia returns, still upset. She takes one or two deep breaths. She takes out her own collar and contemplates putting it on again.
There is a beep from the desk. She replaces the collar in its drawer and presses a button to connect her.

Sylvia Mr Cutler's office, Sylvia speaking . . .

Angelica (*her voice*) Hallo, it's Angelica Stanchion . . . May I speak with Mervyn Cutler, please . . .

Sylvia I'm afraid Mervyn's on holiday at present, Ms Stanchion . . .

Angelica (*her voice*) Oh. I urgently need to speak to him . . .

Sylvia He and his wife are both away till next week. I'm sorry, I did my best to notify all his regular clients, Ms Stanchion . . .

Angelica (*her voice*) It's desperately important. I have to speak to someone . . .

Sylvia May I help at all? If you can tell me the nature of your problem . . .

Angelica (*her voice*) It's extremely personal and private . . . I'm – we're getting married in just under a month . . . at least I hope we are . . . and my fiancé, he's just . . . (*her voice faltering*) he just told me last night . . . that he wants . . . he wants – (*A huge sob*)

Sylvia Just a moment, Ms Stanchion, this does sound rather personal. I'm switching you to confidential mode.

She presses a button.

(*Raising her eyes to heaven, to herself*) Dear God, what now . . .?

She presses another button and continues the call like a normal phone call via her internal inbuilt receiver.

(*Continuing*) That's better . . . carry on . . . yes, of course . . . of course . . . (*Sympathetically*) Mmm . . . mmm . . . oh dear, that does sound worrying for you . . . yes, I can imagine alarm bells would indeed be ringing . . . Look, Ms Stanchion, I think you really should wait until Mervyn . . . No, I'm certain he'll be able to advise you . . . No, pre-marital liability, that's very much his speciality . . . No, if you're looking to take out nuptial protection insurance . . . Yes, full UAD – Unusual Abnormal Demands . . . Yes, they're all covered . . . Totally comprehensive . . . *Very* much his territory, yes . . . no,

Mervyn's certainly the person to talk to . . . Yes, I do, I think it certainly would be the best . . . Well, I'm no expert, Ms Stanchion, but your fiancé's demands do seem very . . . yes . . . Including her veil? . . . his mother's, you say? Well, there's sentimentality and then there's sentimentality, isn't there? . . . yes . . . shoes, yes . . . Yes . . . underwear, naturally . . . yes . . . mmm . . . Mmm . . . sprang it on you, last night, yes . . . just like that . . . No, it does sound as if he planned it rather carefully, Ms Stanchion . . . yes . . . yes, of course you do . . . Well, it's *your* day . . . yes, your *big* day, surely? . . . And with the two of you in white . . . yes . . . no, I've never been married, not personally, no . . . no . . . I think you do need to put it on hold, if you can . . . Wait until Mervyn's back at his desk . . . Yes, I'm sure he'll sort it out for you, one way or another . . . I promise he'll make it his first priority . . . Yes, I will, Ms Stanchion. Yes . . . and good luck!

She presses a button.
More beeps.

God! Poor woman.

Jan comes cautiously into the office. He seems a little less assured than previously. He is no longer in his uniform but dressed in an elegant suit. Both mentally and physically his android elements have become more evident.

Jan Sylvia . . .

Sylvia (*startled*) Jan! Goodness. I haven't seen you for – ages and ages!

Jan Ten years, to the exact day . . .

Sylvia Of course, Lorraine's leaving party?

Jan Correct.

Sylvia Some party.

Jan Oh, yes.

Sylvia No one left standing, was there?

Jan Except for me.

Sylvia Except for you. That's the way to retire, isn't it?

Jan Is that how you plan to leave, Sylvia?

Sylvia Well, I've a few years to go yet . . . So what brings you to the fifty-ninth floor, Jan? Is Lorraine with you?

Jan She's upstairs on the sixtieth. Visiting former colleagues. Yes, I must admit, like her, I miss it all sometimes. The good old days of S & M.

Sylvia (*startled*) I'm sorry?

Jan Security and Maintenance.

Sylvia Oh, of course. Well, I'm pleased you came down to say hallo to me, Jan. How on earth did you know I'd transferred here?

Jan I didn't.

Sylvia Then how did you –?

Jan I came to see Mr Cutler. I had no idea you were working here, Sylvia.

Sylvia Oh. It wasn't me you've come to see at all?

Jan No. I came to see Mr Cutler.

Sylvia Well, he's not here, I'm afraid. He's on holiday with his family. He won't be back till next week.

Jan Ah. I did not have that information. Being no longer employed here, I am no longer connected to the system. Otherwise I would have known. I'm so sorry. Excuse me.

Jan makes to leave.

Sylvia Just a minute, Jan! Don't leave!

Jan stops.

What do you want to see Mr Cutler for?

Jan (*uneasily*) It is – it is a personal matter.

Sylvia I see. To do with marriage?

Jan Yes.

Sylvia Your marriage?

Jan It is a personal matter. Lorraine and I are still very much in love.

Sylvia Good.

Jan Fifty years and never an argument.

Sylvia Wonderful. Very few can say that.

Jan I hope it is rewarding work, assisting Mr Cutler.

Sylvia It's – different.

A slight pause.

Jan Lorraine and I, we are still very much in love, you know.

Sylvia Yes, you said. I'm very happy for you both.

Jan Marital liability must be an interesting area in which to work?

Sylvia Yes. It can be.

Jan Filled with challenge, I imagine. Marriage is a complex institution. Filled with outs and ins. Lorraine and I, we have no arguments. None at all.

A slight pause.

Sylvia Jan, is there a problem? Is something wrong?

Jan Nothing. I am functioning perfectly normally, Sylvia.

Sylvia I'm sorry, I didn't mean to . . .

Jan Perfectly normally. Considering my age. Mustn't complain. (*He laughs*) Lorraine and I, we are still very much in love, you know.

Sylvia Jan, we don't deal with problems inside marriage, not here.

Jan No?

Sylvia That's altogether different, you see, you need . . . All we do here, all Mr Cutler deals with is pre-marriage, you see. People who are contemplating marriage or civil relationship contracts sometimes consult us, particularly if they're wealthy or have wealthy parents, in order to protect them from exploitation or abuse. Financially. It used to be purely financial. To protect them from unreasonable settlements in the case of premature separation. But recently it's tending to include mental and physical demands as well.

Jan I see. (*Puzzled*) Physical?

Sylvia Well, I won't go into details, but people do, in a marriage, demand rather a lot from each other sometimes, which occasionally entails – unanticipated Health and Safety issues. And not just in the bedroom, either. You'd be amazed what some people insist their future partner agrees never to indulge in. Everything from eating meat to oral sex. You'd be amazed. So unless it's something in that line . . .

Jan I don't eat meat.

Sylvia No.

Jan Indeed, I don't eat at all. Except socially.

Sylvia No.

Jan And as for –

Sylvia No. Quite.

Jan Ours is a marriage of companionship, you understand? We have no arguments –

Sylvia Yes, you don't need to explain, Jan . . .

Jan Lorraine needs a cuddle, occasionally, you see. And a good cry now and then –

Sylvia Honestly, Jan, you don't have to go into details, if you –

Jan (*continuing, now unstoppable*) The cuddles, I am happily able to provide. And the crying is considerably less frequent than it was.

Sylvia Then what's the problem?

Jan In recent years I have this increasing sense of – inadequacy, Sylvia. That is the only way I can describe it.

Sylvia Inadequacy? How?

Jan Over the past months I have been increasingly forced to compensate.

Sylvia Compensate, how?

Jan She needs – Lorraine needs –

Sylvia What is it she needs, Jan? What does Lorraine need?

Jan She needs – this may sound like a criticism of her and I in no way wish to criticise her, you understand – but she requires – almost invariably to be in the right. And in many cases and with increased frequency with advancing age, she is not, you see. She is most certainly in the wrong.

Sylvia I see. I think, Jan, you need sometimes to make allowances. Agree with things she says that you probably don't agree with. It's called rubbing along together. Lorraine probably does the same to you. She agrees with things you say that she knows in her heart are wrong.

Jan No, you see Lorraine doesn't need to.

Sylvia She doesn't?

Jan No. Because everything I say is invariably correct. I am a model twelve modified. I have a built-in zero point zero, zero six margin of error.

Sylvia Oh dear. That is a problem.

Jan (*pouring it all out to her*) But Lorraine will simply not accept that. I try to adjust. My programming allows me to concede in disagreements where I am *almost* certainly in the right and she is *almost* certainly in the wrong. I have an inbuilt tolerance to accommodate that. But in cases when she is definitely wrong and I am totally right, then to concede is tantamount to an untruth. And you will appreciate I am allowed very little leeway for lying. It is contrary to my entire main system. I am being forced to tell so many lies that my main routines are gradually being corroded.

Sylvia Oh, that's not good, is it? You should see someone about it, Jan. A doc— No, well. An expert.

Jan You mean a technician? But if I went to see a technician, that would only cause Lorraine to worry, you see. I would not want to upset her. If I was forced to leave her for any length of time in order to undergo an extensive overhaul, she would be lost without me. We are still very much in love. This evening, for instance, I have arranged a romantic dinner for two at her favourite restaurant. A special birthday dinner.

Sylvia Even though you don't eat?

Jan I will go through the motions, as usual.

Lorraine enters.

Lorraine Oh, here you are, darling . . .

Jan Ah!

Lorraine I wondered where you were. I wish you'd tell me where you're going, darling, instead of just wandering off like that. Someone said they'd seen you coming in here. What are you doing in here, dearest?

Jan I – I –

Sylvia He came to visit me. Hallo, Lorraine . . .

Lorraine registers Sylvia's presence for the first time.

Lorraine What – ? (*With a cry of delight*) Sylvia! Is it Sylvia? Dear girl! It must be Sylvia? How lovely!

Sylvia (*rising*) Hallo, Lorraine . . .

The two embrace each other, long-lost friends.

Been a long time . . .

Lorraine It's been ages and ages . . . How are you? Let me look at you. Oh, you look just the same. Same dear little Sylvia . . . You've not changed a jot.

Sylvia Nor have you.

Lorraine Oh, darling, I've gone completely to seed. Don't even look at me. A hundred and ten today, darling, would you believe it? Tell you what, we're just on our way out for an early dinner – I can't eat late these days, not possibly – Why don't you come and join us both?

Sylvia (*uncertainly*) Well, I –

Lorraine You must come. It's my birthday. A hundred and ten! Can you believe that? You must come! It'll be like old times. She must, mustn't she, Jan?

Jan I have reserved a table for two, darling . . .

Lorraine Well, it's easy enough to change it, surely?

Jan They appeared to be extremely busy.

Lorraine Oh, well, they always say that and then when you turn up, the place is half empty. Come on, Sylvia, I absolutely insist you join us.

Sylvia No, I honestly don't think l can, Lorraine, not this evening. We're snowed under here at present . . .

Lorraine I won't take no, Sylvia. I insist. It's my hundred and tenth birthday and I insist! You can't spoil my birthday, can she, Jan?

Sylvia is a little torn.

Sylvia (*with a glance at Jan*) Alright then, I – I'll just have to check first with Mervyn. Whether it's alright for me to leave early – (*Indicating the inner office*) I need to go and check with Mervyn.

Jan (*puzzled*) I understood he was –

Sylvia If he says it's alright, I'd love to join you, Lorraine. Won't be a moment. He's in there busy with a client – or else I'm sure he'd be out to say – (*Calling gently*) Mr Cutler! May I come in for a second?

Sylvia goes off.

Lorraine Tell him it's my hundred and tenth birthday! He has to let you come.

Jan (*mystified*) Most extraordinary . . .

Lorraine Don't fret, darling. They'll find us a bigger table. Or else lay an extra place. You worry too much, darling, don't you? Old worrier, aren't you?

Jan I had hoped, darling, it would be just us two. A special celebration.

Lorraine Where are we going, anyway? Or is it going to be a surprise?

Jan No. It's the usual. Where we went last year. Where we usually go. Your favourite.

Lorraine Where's that?

Jan The Caraboose.

Lorraine The Caraboose? I loathe the Caraboose.

Jan No you don't, darling, you –

Lorraine I detest it. It's far too noisy and they always have that deafening band.

Jan But you enjoyed dancing to them last year, didn't you?

Lorraine Dancing? Me? Nonsense. I don't even like dancing . . .

Jan appears to be experiencing an internal struggle.

Jan Yes – you – darling – you – I – I – I'll go ahead and get us a taxi, darling.

Jan hurries out.

Lorraine (*after him as he goes*) We don't need a taxi, for heaven's sake. It's only just round the corner . . . (*Laughing*) Dear oh dear, honestly! That man!

Sylvia returns.

Sylvia (*calling behind her as she comes*) Thank you. Sorry to have disturbed you, Mervyn.

Lorraine (*expectantly*) Well?

Sylvia He says no, he's terribly sorry, Lorraine. He can't possibly spare me. Not this evening.

Lorraine Oh, for God's sake, let me have a word with the man –

Sylvia No, Lorraine, please, don't! He's with an important client. Where's Jan?

Lorraine He's gone off in search of a taxi, would you believe? Ridiculous man.

Sylvia He seems very fond of you.

Lorraine Yes, and I adore him, bless him. But he does drive me mad sometimes. He gets so nit-picky and meticulous . . . Now tell me, how are you, Sylvia? Still happy? Are you still with your deep-sea diver?

Sylvia My who? Oh, him. That was ages ago. No, we split up. Years ago.

Lorraine Oh dear. I am sorry. (*Sympathetically*) All on your own now, darling? Poor little Sylvia. Never mind, you'll find someone, dear. Eventually.

Sylvia (*swiftly*) No, I'm fine. I have someone. I'm perfectly fine, Lorraine.

Lorraine Oh, have you? Who?

Sylvia Well, he's a – he's a space pilot, actually.

Lorraine Good Lord! Really?

Sylvia Which means he's away rather a lot, of course. Cargo, you know. Transporting Marsh Puppies and things. Mars mostly. Venus. Sometimes Jupiter. The outer moons, you know.

Lorraine (*genuinely amazed*) Good heavens above! I never knew that! You never told me. A pilot? How glamorous. Where on earth do you meet these people, Sylvia?

Jan returns.

Jan There is a taxi waiting downstairs, darling.

Lorraine We don't need a taxi, darling, I've said. It's only round the corner.

Jan It's a little bit of a walk for you, darling. There is also a sixty per cent possibility of precipitation . . .

Lorraine Precipitation? Don't be so silly, it's not going to rain, darling . . .

Jan (*opening and closing his mouth*) Silly me . . . (*He laughs*)

Lorraine Silly you! (*She laughs*)

Sylvia laughs nervously with them. In the midst of the merriment Jan's laugh changes to a warning whooping sound.

Sylvia (*alarmed*) Jan!

Lorraine (*alarmed*) Darling!

Lorraine thumps Jan on the back. The noise stops.

Jan (*recovering*) Thank you, darling.

Sylvia Is he alright?

Lorraine He keeps having those. I keep on at him to see a mechanic but he flatly refuses to see one. No point in arguing with him, either. Save your breath. See you soon, Sylvia.

Sylvia Bye, Lorraine. Take care.

Lorraine goes out. Jan lingers.

Goodbye, Jan.

Jan Goodbye, Sylvia.

Lorraine (*off, calling*) Now where on earth have you got to? Jan!

Jan We are still very much in love.

Jan hurries out after Lorraine.
Sylvia sits, deep in thought.
From outside, a rumble of thunder.

Sylvia (*glancing out*) Oh dear . . .

She remains at her desk while the lights cross-fade to Titus's office.
His Hipro is beeping again.
Titus hurries on to answer it. He stabs the desk button.
Grace, an older version, appears on the Hipro. Time and expensive cosmetic assistance have treated her extremely well. She remains very youthfully dressed in her chic exercise gear.

Titus (*expecting Franklin*) Ah. Grace.

Grace Ty. I need to talk to you.

Titus I'm listening . . .

Grace I – sorry, I'm a bit hot and sweaty. Just been working out on the low-grav machine – they're amazing, these new ones, you know, you really ought to try them sometime, Ty – there's this one which hurls you right up, incredibly high . . . you know, at least twenty metres –

Titus Yes, Grace. I'm sure it's amazing. What did you want to talk about?

Grace Yes. (*Pause*) I wanted to talk to you – without Daddy – being – I mean – I don't know how to say this, really. Ty, I think we ought to separate. Don't you?

A pause.

Yeah. That's it basically. Really. Yeah. (*Pause*) Really. (*She squirms uncomfortably*)

Titus You think we ought to separate?

Grace Yeah. Live apart. You know. Don't you think?

Titus We already do live apart, Grace. Most of the time, we do.

Grace Yeah. I know we do, but . . .

Titus So what are you proposing that's new, Grace? Are you suggesting we divorce?

Grace No, not exactly . . . you know . . . perhaps we ought to just stop being married for a bit . . .

Titus You mean we divorce?

Grace Just temporarily.

Titus (*angrily*) Grace, you can't be temporarily divorced. We're either married or we're not.

Grace (*tearfully*) Don't shout! You don't need to shout over these things, Ty. You always shout!

Titus I'm sorry.

Grace (*sulkily*) Whenever I try and talk about – us – the future . . . you just yell and get all cross . . . and grumpy.

Titus I'm sorry. I apologise. (*Calmly*) You're asking for a divorce, Grace? Is that it?

Grace Well . . . (*She hesitates*)

Titus Yes or no?

Grace Well . . . (*She hesitates again*)

Titus (*quietly*) Yes or no?

Grace Well . . .

Titus (*loudly*) YES OR NO, GRACE?

Grace (*equally loudly*) YES, I DO! I WANT A DIVORCE!

Silence.

Titus Alright.

Grace What? (*Pause*) You want a divorce, too?

Titus If that's what you want.

Grace That's not fair. I only want one if you want one.

Titus I only want one because I know you want one.

Pause.

Grace It's our anniversary next week. Fifty years. We'll be throwing all those years away, won't we?

Titus Don't think of it as throwing them away . . . think of it as us travelling on.

Grace Time travelling . . . yes. We started out so well, didn't we? You and me? I was going to be this brilliant dancer and you were going to be so wealthy and successful . . . and look what's happened . . .

Titus I am wealthy and successful . . .

Grace You're not successful . . .

Titus Yes, I am, I'm the vice-chief executive of HEA, I call that successful.

Grace No, you're not, you're just working for Daddy, that's all.

Titus does not reply.

Daddy's the one who's wealthy and successful.

Titus Yes. Of course, you're perfectly right, Grace.

A slight pause.

(*Thinking to terminate the conversation*) Well . . .

Grace I'm sixty-seven next November.

Titus These days that's young.

Grace I could never believe I'd ever be sixty-six.

Titus I'm sixty-eight. The same age I was when I came back to visit you that time. When I travelled back.

Grace Oh, yes. The day it all changed. I think that's part of the problem, Ty.

Titus That you now regret it? Our marriage?

Grace No, I would still have married you, Ty. I won't ever regret that. That's not what I'm saying . . .

Titus What exactly is your problem, Grace?

Grace It's – it's difficult . . . I loved you so much then. You were eighteen. I was sixteen. I loved you so much. So very much. Only you came back, looking like you are now. You travelled back from now to warn me, didn't you? Not to accept Daddy's money but –

Titus (*growing impatient again*) Yes, I know all this, Grace. I was there, wasn't I? Twice, I was there . . .

Grace Yes, but don't you see. I met *you*. You as you are now, the sixty-eight-year-old you. Not the eighteen-year-old that I was in love with then. I saw this old – I'm sorry this is so hurtful, Ty, I don't mean it to be – I saw this *old* man. Like you are now. Only now you're even more worn out and sadder –

Titus Grace, that was fifty years ago – you couldn't ask me to stay the same age for ever –

Grace No, that's not what I'm saying either –

Titus For God's sake, you've grown older as well. We've both of us grown older, Grace!

Grace Yes, but we haven't grown older together, have we? That's the point. When people spend their lives together things happen gradually so they don't even notice the changes happening to them, most of the time. That's the way it's meant to happen. But I'd already seen the future, Ty. I'd seen what you'd be like fifty years from then. And it just – started giving me nightmares. I could see my future. Our future. Do you understand what I'm saying?

Titus Yes. I gave you nightmares. Thanks.

Grace No, no. It's not you . . . It's just we're not supposed to see what's ahead of us. Life's meant to be a surprise, Ty. Every day should be unexpected. Some days are awful, other days, that you never expect to be, turn out to be just wonderful. But we're not supposed to know about tomorrow, you see? Otherwise it's all so – I don't know – disappointing.

A silence.

Titus I came back fifty years ago and you didn't want me then. You said no thanks, I'll take my chance with someone my own age. And the irony is that, now that I am your age, you don't want me now, either.

Grace Do you still want me?

Titus Oh, yes. I still want you. But then you've scarcely altered, Grace, have you? You've never really grown up. All these years, day after day, I've been seeing myself growing older and older. Watching you stay exactly the same.

Grace If you only knew what it cost to stay like this . . . I was frightened, Ty. Please try to understand. I saw the future and I was just terrified. I must go, now. I think Daddy's calling. I think he needs me. Bye, bye, Gorgeous.

She disconnects before he can say another word. She goes.

Titus (*softly, to himself*) Bye, Gracious. Go back to your successful daddy.

Titus sits at his desk for a moment, sinking his head into his hands.

Lights come up on Sylvia, also still sitting at her desk. A moment.

Titus comes to a decision. He opens the drawer and takes out his collar. He takes a deep breath. Puts it on and stabs a button on the desk. He stands in the doorway, struggling to control himself.

The virtual bar appears again. Bellina, as usual, is standing behind it. Music and effects as before.

Bellina (*seeing Fabiano approach*) Hey! The man's back in town!

Fabiano enters. He lacks his usual swagger and exuberance, reflecting Titus's own uncertain mood.

Titus (*tearfully*) Hallo . . .

Fabiano (*tearfully*) Hallo . . .

Bellina Hey, big guy! Welcome back to *In Your Dreams*. What'll it be? Your usual?

Titus (*weakly*) . . . please . . .

Fabiano (*weakly*) . . . please . . .

Bellina (*unaware of his mood, preparing his drink*) So where you been, man, since we last saw you? Ganymede? Callisto? Or did you make it all the way to Titan? Hey, those rings! Close up they must be spectacular! (*Giving him his drink*) There you go, one double Comet's Tail. Warm beds, soft landings, feller!

Titus (*sobbing*) Warm beds . . . soft . . . soft . . . (*Suddenly, falling to his knees by his desk*) Oh, God, I can't do this, I'm sorry!

Fabiano (*falling to his knees by the bar, sobbing*) . . . I can't do this, I'm sorry!

Bellina Hey, hey, big guy . . . something wrong? What's wrong?

Fabiano (*sobbing*) . . . sorry . . . I'm sorry . . . I can't do this!

Bellina (*alarmed*) What's with my favourite spaceman, huh . . .? What's the trouble, big guy?

Fabiano (*beside himself with grief*) I'm sorry, I'm just . . . I just need . . .

Bellina Hey – hey – hey – now, steady, feller . . . Just a minute, stay right there! I'll call your favourite girl. I'll call Seraphina . . .

She presses a concealed button under the shelf. Correspondingly, in Sylvia's office, there is a beep from her collar, waking her from her reverie. Though also distressed, she seems now filled with new determination. She rises.

Bellina (*during this, to Fabiano*) Hey listen, Fabiano . . . Tonight, I saved room nine for you. You know, the big double? With that great bed? And the view over the bay. Not that you two'll be admiring the view, huh?

Bellina laughs. Fabiano and Titus sob.

Sylvia (*angrily*) Right! Enough of this! Quite enough!

She puts on her own collar and, taking a deep breath, presses the button to activate it.

Listen, just hold it together, feller, I've called Seraphina, she'll be here soon . . . She'll cheer you up, wait and see . . .

Seraphina arrives, again mirroring Sylvia.

(*Seeing her, with relief*) Hey! What did I say? Here's the beautiful little lady . . . Come and cheer up your space boy, dream girl!

Sylvia (*aggressively*) Why? What's the matter with him . . .

Seraph (*aggressively*) Why? What's the matter with him . . .

Sylvia . . . fallen out of his stupid spaceship again, has he?

Seraph . . . fallen out of his stupid spaceship again, has he?

Bellina Hey . . . hey . . .

Over the next section, both principals' and their avatars' voices are in precise unison.

Seraph
Sylvia } (*together*) What's wrong, big man, been bitten by a Venusian Marsh Puppy, have you?

Fabiano
Titus } (*together, wailing*) Oh, leave me alone! Just leave me alone!

Bellina Hey, hey, Seraphina! Easy now, sweetheart!

Seraph
Sylvia } (*together*) And don't call me that . . . my name is not Seraphina!

Bellina What gives round here? Seraphina! Fabiano!

Titus
Fabiano } (*together, to Bellina*) Leave us alone, for God's sake, Bellina, please?

Both avatars and their principals now turn to their opposite number. Fabiano faces Sylvia, Titus faces Seraphina.

Seraph
Sylvia } (*together*) We need to talk, don't we?

Bellina Talk? You two?

Fabiano
Titus } (*together*) Yes, we do. We need to talk.

Bellina (*laughing*) What the hell do you two have to *talk* about – ?

Fabiano
Titus } (*together, sharply*) Oh, shut up, Bellina! Just shut the fuck up, will you!

Seraph
Sylvia } (*together, more quietly*) Please, Bellina.

Bellina (*slightly huffy*) Alright, two minutes. First trouble, it's upstairs. Sort it out there, not in my bar, right?

She goes off behind the bar.
A slight pause.

Seraph
Sylvia } (*together*) We need to talk about us.

Fabiano
Titus } (*together*) You and me?

Seraph
Sylvia } (*together*) I need to know who you are. The real you.

Bellina (*her offstage voice, sensing danger*) Be careful, folks, you're stepping outside the safety rules here . . .

Titus Alright. My real name is Titus – Titus Armitage . . .

Seraph
Sylvia } (*together*) Titus . . .

Titus . . . I'm an executive with the time travel firm, HEA . . . I'm married. Correction, I was married until a few moments ago . . . I . . . I'm sixty-eight years old but I'm told I look older than that and I . . . I . . . (*Tailing off, apologetically*) . . . I'm afraid that's all there is to me, really. And you? What about you?

Sylvia My name is Sylvia. I'm a PA working for Garbett Downside in the Pre-Marital Liability Department. I'm eighty years old and not in the least beautiful. I have no one in my life and I'm slowly dying of loneliness. Won't you help me please, Titus, whoever you are . . .? (*In almost a whisper*) . . . help me . . . help me . . . please . . .

Seraphina continues to reflect Sylvia's desperation. Titus stares at her. Fabiano stares at Sylvia.

Sylvia
Seraph } (*together*) . . . help me . . . please . . . (*A final urgent cry*) PLEASE . . .

Bellina (*her voice*) Protocols illegally breached. This *In Your Dreams* session is now terminating, folks. One minute to closedown.

An alarm starts to beep as the programme begins to shut down.

Seraphina and Titus slowly move closer in time to the beeping alarm. Sylvia and Titus do the same. The couples no longer speak simultaneously but separately again, as the programme begins to shut down.

Fabiano (*moving to her, gently*) Sylvia? . . . You say your name is Sylvia?

Sylvia (*moving to him, rather shyly*) Yes . . . Sylvia Joan Wilkins . . .

Seraph (*moving to Titus, rather shyly*) Yes . . . Sylvia Joan Wilkins . . .

Titus (*moving to her, gently*) Sylvia Joan Wilkins . . .

Fabiano (*touching Sylvia's face*) Happy to meet you at last, Sylvia Joan Wilkins. Would you permit Fabiano, please, one final kiss?

Sylvia (*touching his face*) Yes, of course . . . Titus . . .

Seraph (*touching Titus's face*) Fabiano . . .

Titus (*touching her face*) Titus, Titus David Oliver Henry Armitage . . .

The couples kiss. As they do so, the programme finally finishes. The lights fade till only the bar is still dimly lit for a brief moment. Thunder.

Bellina (*her voice*) *In Your Dreams* session is now terminated.

The bar fades out.

(*Her voice fading away*) Aw, what the hell, you win some, you lose some . . .

Lightning. Thunder. When the lights return, Fabiano and Seraphina have gone.

Sylvia and Titus remain in the same positions but are now standing on opposite sides of a street.

It is raining and there is a distant whine of electro-traffic.

Both are looking around them. They have clearly arranged to meet and are uncertain what the other looks like.

Both see each other at the same moment.

Titus (*calling tentatively*) Sylvia . . .?

Sylvia (*calling tentatively*) Titus . . .?

Titus indicates a place they can take shelter. They both make a dash for it.

Titus (*slightly breathless*) Sylvia Joan Wilkins . . .?

Sylvia (*likewise*) Yes. Titus David Oliver Henry Armitage . . .?

Titus Guilty. How do you do?

Both extend their hands instinctively to touch the other's cheek. Then, realising that they are both the real thing and not avatars, they opt for shaking hands. They smile at each other, rather shyly.

You lied to me, you know, Ms Wilkins.

Sylvia I did?

Titus You are, you're beautiful.

Sylvia So are you, Mr Armitage. So are you.

He draws her towards him gently and puts his other arm round her. Sylvia responds. They cling on, unaware of the world around them. Music creeps under.

(*Nestling into his arms*) Oh, this is good . . . this is so good . . .

More thunder. The rain continues. They remain happily together as the lights fade to a blackout.